THE CAGED ONES

ASIAN
PORTRAITS

VISAGES
D'ASIE

THE CAGED ONES

Ludu U Hla

Translated from Burmese
by *Sein Tu*

Illustrated by
U Wa Thone

Orchid Press
Bangkok 1998

Ludu U Hla (1910-1982)
THE CAGED ONES
First English edition 1986
Reprinted 1998
Original title in Burmese:
Hlaung-chaine-hte-ga-nhet-nge-myar

Orchid Press
98/13 Soi Apha Phirom, Ratchada Road,
Chatuchak, Bangkok 10900, Thailand

ISBN 974-8299-15-5

Ludu U Hla

Foreword

Ludu U Hla (1910 - 1982)

U Hla was born in a middle class land-owning family of Nyaunglebin in lower Burma. He started publishing a monthly youth magazine named *Kyipwa yay* ("Progress for Youth") in 1933 and this magazine continued until the outbreak of the second World War. He was married in 1939 to a young budding author from Mandalay, Daw Amar, and they had five children and four grandchildren.

During the war, U Hla translated Ashihae Hino's "War and Soldier" into Burmese, and published it as the first book ever published during the Fascist occupation.

When the war was over, he started the fortnightly journal *Ludu,* which means "The People", and it is from this time his pen-name Ludu U Hla originated. Then in 1946 he began publishing the "Ludu Daily News", which continued until 1967 when it ceased publication.

Ludu U Hla collected around 2,000 folktales of the indigenous peoples of Burma, and in his lifetime published approximately 1,500 folktales in a total of 43 books. In 1963, his collection of Arakanese folktales was awarded the prestigious Burmese "Sarpay Beikman Literary Award".

Besides the collection of folktales, he wrote another 54 books, nine of which were biographies of prisoners he met when he was jailed on five occasions for political reasons in the 1940's and 1950's. He left over 500 unpublished folktales and seven unfinished manuscripts to his wife.

His works in Burmese include *The Life of Kalidasa* (3 vols.), *Newspapers as History, With the Wind, Labour heroes I have known, Japanese Journey, To My Wife and Children from Jail, Nightime in Mandalay, Indonesia from East to West,* as well as works on drug addiction, alcoholism, and the rice and timber trades.

Ludu U Hla wrote all his books in Burmese, and is well known as an author who wrote a simple, direct, and easily understandable Burmese, and this comes through also in translations of his writings.

The following of his works have been translated.

1. *Folktales of Burma*, translated by K. Mandalay, 1972, 1979, 210 pp.
2. *The Victim*, translated by U Than Tun and Kathleen Forbes, Mandalay, 1973, 282 pp.
3. *Tales of Indigenous People of Burma*, translated by U Than Tun. Mandalay, 1974, pp. (Japanese translation published in Tokyo, 1976).
4. *Märchen des Völker Burmas*, translated by Annemarie Esche. Leipzig, 1975, 550 pp.
5. *Ckazku Hapodob Supubi* ("Tales of the Peoples of Burma"), unauthorized translation into Russian, compiled by V.B. Kasevich and Y.M. Osipor with an introduction by D.V. Deopik. Nauka Press, Moscow, 1976, 592 pp.
6. *More Favourite Stories from Burma*, translated by Kathleen Forbes. Singapore, 1978, 62 pp.
7. *Prince of Rubies and Other Folktales from Burma*, translated by U Than Tun and Kathleen Forbes. Mandalay, 1980, 309 pp. (Bilingual edition).
8. *Märchen aus Burma*, translated by Marie Louise Hitz and Walter Klinger. Bonn, 1980, 269 pp.
9. *With the Wind*, translated into Japanese by Shiz o Ka toda. Tokyo, 1982.
10. Selections of Folktales collected by Ludu U Hla have appeared in *Collection of Asia Short Stories*, 1981 and the Japanese editions of *Folktales of the World*, translated by Ono Toru.

Hlaung-chaine-hte-ga-nghet-nge-myar ("The Caged Ones") was first published in Burmese and won the UNESCO Award for 1958. This is the first translation into English. In "The Caged Ones" the author outlines with sympathy and compassion the life history of sixteen young prisoners whom he met in Rangoon Central Jail. Told in their own words, these stories document in detail the social pressures and circumstances which drove these unfortunate adolescents to a life outside the Law.

VIII

As the world in 1985 will celebrate the International Youth Year (IYY), this book may provide a reminder to all of us who are fortunate to live in freedom and security that we have special responsibilities towards all youth, no matter at which end of the socio-economic scale they were born. Ludu U Hla, in the introduction to *The Victim*, summed up his reasons for writing so extensively about prisoners, and no doubt the young ones were uppermost in his mind when he wrote:

> "Because I have written a lot about the prisoners, I do not want the reader to assume that I am wholly on the side of the criminals. But what I wish to make clear is that though they may commit atrocious crimes, they are not animals. I strongly believe that they should have a chance to be reaccepted among their fellow citizens should they repent."

Rangoon, May 1984.   H. K. Kulöy.

Contents

Preface

In a narrow cell measuring ten feet by seven are several youthful prisoners. Within the narrow confines of these walls they may be observed playing, singing, wrestling, clowning, and occasionally, fighting. Sometimes they are very noisy and boisterous. At other times they are silent and morose.

At 6 o'clock every morning the cell door is thrown wide open and they are then free to emerge and stretch their cramped limbs. At 6 p.m. the massive iron door of the cell clangs shut on them and they are left to spend the night in each other's company and that of a stinking chamber pot standing on the corner.

The slamming of the door is followed by dead silence. After a while conversation starts up again. Somebody begins singing. Before long swearing is heard, followed by the sounds of quarrelling. There is laughter, and there are tears, and finally, silence.

*

The material presented in the following pages was gathered during the years 1954 to 1956, when I was a political prisoner held in Rangoon Central Jail. People have often asked me why I undertook this task in the first place. In answer I can only refer them to my state of mind at that time.

Imagine yourself to be imprisoned in a jail located hundreds of miles away from your home town. It is hardly feasible for your family, your parents and your other relatives to uproot themselves and move to this distant city just to be near you. As it is, they have enough worries of their own trying to make both ends meet during your absence. The children's schooling also has to be taken into account.

Frequent trips to see you are out of the question and there is no point in prolonging each visit as nothing further can be done to obtain your release. In three years and three months your wife has been able to visit you only three times. Each time she comes she brings one of the children to see their father. The youngest child does not even remember you. Under these circumstances, is it any wonder that your sympathies are aroused at the plight of the young boys you find in prison, many of whom are no older than your own sons?.

Suppose further that you are a political prisoner and that you are not permitted to have visitors other than the members of your immediate family and a few other close relatives. Some of those who can see you stay away for fear of political reprisals. There are only two visiting days in a week and the visits, when they do take place are very short indeed, usually lasting only from fifteen minutes to half an hour. Wouldn't you decide that your life for the moment must be bound by the four walls of the prison and that your interests must necessarily be so circumscribed?.

Why have these young people found themselves in jail? A prison is not the proper place for those of such tender years. And why are there so many of them? Troubled by these thoughts I began to interview several of these boys to try to elicit their life stories and if possible to find out where they went wrong. I sincerely believe that the accounts given in the following pages are substantially correct.

The number of people interested in youth affairs is happily on the increase. Unfortunately the youth problem also is becoming even more complex and we need all the help available in trying to solve it. It is my earnest hope that this book will prove useful not only to social workers and officials, but to all those who are trying to gain a better understanding of the adolescent and the pressures which drive him towards a life of crime.

Mandalay,
10 January 1958

Ludu U Hla

I
UNREQUITED LOVE

In Rangoon jail he was known as Nga Khwe as well as Salay. How was it possible that such a good natured person could be serving a sentence for murder?.

His duty in the prison was to carry meals to the inmates of Cell Block 13. This was a very arduous task and avoided by most prisoners. The rice had to be placed on a small hand cart and lugged to the dining room. Then another trip had to be made, carrying the heavy curry pot on one's shoulders. If the hand cart was out of order, the rice itself had to be similarly transported. Although usually enough food was prepared, there were times when more was needed and then a further trip had to be hurriedly made to the kitchen. When all the prisoners had eaten, Nga Khwe had to clear the tables and wash the plates and dishes. None of the others used to take their duties as seriously as Nga Khwe.

In the evening Nga Khwe would clean a bucket and take it to the night shift in the kitchen to be filled with boiled rice and curry. At 5 a.m. this food had to be carried to the inmates of Cell Block 13. On Sundays the prisoners were given green tea after their morning meal at 10 a.m. and Nga Khwe had to fetch the hot water to the dining room in two large containers. Sometimes the boiling water would spill on his feet and he would then do his round of duties for the next few days with huge blisters on his feet.

Prior to the year 1947, each prisoner was allowed only two ounces of meat a fortnight, the meat being boiled and then lightly fried in a little oil. It was only after the pre-independence prison riots of 1947, in which 17 prisoners are said to have lost their lives, that the present privileges were accorded them. Now prisoners are given pork (or fish) curry every Friday, green tea on Sundays and the right to have food sent in by relatives from outside. They are also permitted to *read newspapers and magazines.*

In December 1951, Rangoon Central Jail was designated as a model jail. Music lessons were introduced and each cell block was permitted to have one mandolin, one violin, one xylophone and one Burmese brass flute. Schools for instruction in the Buddhist scriptures were also established in each block. In response to demands by the inmates, provision was made for instruction in school subjects as well. Facilities for weight-lifting were introduced. Doctors were also permitted to enter the cell blocks even after hours, to attend to emergency cases.

*

Everyone in Nga Khwe's cell block felt friendly towards him. His good nature, his sincerety and his industry endeared him to all. Whenever a person was not feeling well, Nga Khwe would come and tend to needs, for which he was sometimes rewarded with a cheroot or two, but usually with no more than a word of thanks. It made no difference to him, whether or not he was paid for his services and he would just as willingly answer the next call.

Every evening, after his work was done, Nga Khwe would place an offering of flowers before the picture of Buddha in his cell. If there was no room in the two vases on the altar, he would simply pile the flowers in front of the altar.

*

From the time of the Japanese retreat from Burma during the second world war, there had lived near west Chinatown in Rangoon a rice noodle vendor Ko Thein Maung and his wife Ma Tin Hla. They had no children. One day they managed to get a good worker to help them in their work. This was none other than Nga Khwe. Nga Khwe was barely twenty years old then. At about the same time, another person joined the household. This was a ten year old girl named Ma Khin Than or Than Than.

Nga Khwe's daily duty consisted of going around town and selling the rice noodles prepared by Ko Thein Maung and Ma Tin Hla. He would do this everyday come rain or shine and at the end of each day would faithfully turn in every pya that he had earned. He was given no salary whatsoever, being merely fed and clothed by the couple. He was by way of being just an unpaid slave.

Little Than Than was made to sell sugar-cane cut up into small pieces and stuck on the end of small bamboo sticks. Ko Thein Maung and Ma Tin Hla managed to live comfortably on the earnings of Nga Khwe and Than Than.

In time little Than Than reached the age of puberty and Nga Khwe, who was but human could not help noticing that she was growing into a beauty. Ko Thein Maung and Ma Tin Hla, who regarded Nga Khwe as a harmless simpleton who was not quite right in the head, would tease him, saying "Do your work properly and we will give Than Than to you in marriage when she grows up." Poor Nga Khwe took them at their word and worked harder than ever before. When he returned in the evenings he would go and sit beside Than Than, noting how she was ripening into womanhood. Than Than, not knowing whàt Ko Thein Maung had said to Nga Khwe, remained oblivious of his interest. To her he was just another member of the household.

A year passed and Than Than grew lovelièr than ever. Nga Khwe took to peeping into her room at every opportunity to watch her prettying herself before the mirror. She was no longer required to sell sugar cane and the whole household began living on the proceeds of Nga Khwe's noodle sales. However, Ko Thein Maung and his wife showed no gratitude towards him, but lavished all their attention on Than Than. The little girl who used to sell sugar cane had turned into a sweet commodity herself, up for sale to the highest bidder. The young men of the neighbourhood began to court her, but found that unless they had considerable means their attentions were not welcomed by the couple.

Than Than found that in spite of the fact that she was doing no work she could dress far better than before. On her neck she now wore a necklace of gems, there were gold bangles on each wrist and on her ears were set a pair of valuable earrings. Nga Khwe noticed the change, but in his obtuseness could not decide whether they had been purchased from his earnings or not. Nevertheless he saw that they made her even more beautiful and in his heart he rejoiced.

Time passed and Nga Khwe began to grow impatient. One day upon returning home from work, he could control himself no longer and taking his courage in his hands, went up to Ko Thein Maung and Ma Tin Hla and said "You promised to give Than Than to me in marriage when she comes of age. She is already grown up and I want her now." The couple, had had their fun in teasing Nga Khwe by promising Than Than to him. Now they became incensed at what they considered to be insolence on the part of one whom they regarded as a fool and little better than a beast of burden. "What!" they shouted. "Do you realize what you are saying?. Do you think that you are of her station?. You are a cur and a cur should know its place. You can leave this house and leave it immediately!" So saying they drove Nga Khwe out, not even allowing him to take his pitifully scant belongings with him.

When this matter became generally known in the neighbourhood, everyone took pity on Nga Khwe and went out of their way to be kind to him. The young men, who knew certain things which Nga Khwe was ignorant of, were especially sorry for him. They knew that while Nga Khwe had been out all day everyday slaving for Ko Thein Maung and his wife, a rich Chinese driving a big Packard had been calling on Than Than regularly. It was after the advent of this Chinese that the girl began to blossom with jewelry. At first he used to come only for an hour or so, but after a while he began to stay for two or three hours. On his earlier visits he contented himself with chatting with Ko Thein Maung and Ma Tin Hla in the front room, stealing brief glances at Than Than only when she brought in tea for them. After a while Than Than began joining them in the front room. Before long Than Than and the Chinese could be seen sitting by themselves engaged in conversation. Finally there came a time when the two of them disappeared into the back room and only the big Packard remained in front of the house.

Nga Khwe had known nothing of this. By the time he return- ed home each day, the Chinese had already left the house. In the mornings he was in a hurry to get on the street with his rice-noodles and had to eat alone, but his evening meals were usually taken in the company of Than Than and the others. At these times his happiness knew no bounds, and he hardly knew what curries he was eating. Now and then he felt a passing wish that he could buy her a small pre- sent, but since he had no money of his own he realised that as soon as Ko Thein Maung saw any present, he would know that Nga Khwe had been stealing from the rice-noodle money.

When Nga Khwe was driven out from Ko Thein Maung's house, he was given shelter by various families in the neighbourhood.

Because of his habit of helping with the household chores, he found himself very popular with the housewives, who fed him food which was as good if not better than that he had previously had. Nevertheless, at the end of one week Nga Khwe had grown thin and haggard.

In the hope of seeing Than Than's face, he would walk past her house at least ten times a day. It was only then that he noticed the big saloon car parked in front of her house. He also saw her in the company of the Chinese and saw how intimate they seemed to be. While he himself, after all those years of faithful service had been driven from the house, he noticed that the Chinese was always given an effusive welcome, not only by Ko Thein Maung and Ma Tin Hla but by Than Than as well. The young men in the neighbourhood explained the situation to Nga Khwe and encouraged him to try and see Than Than and plead his cause with her. Taking this advice, Nga Khwe one day entered the house when she was alone and declared his love for her. Than Than however, had come to consider somebody like him to be beneath her station. She had been taught to expect the best from life and Nga Khwe could, in her eyes, in no way compare with the rich and well-dressed young men she wanted. Accordingly, his halting attempts to change her mind fell upon deaf ears and she spurned him, saying "Go away! Are you mad?. I don't want to hear this kind of talk from you any more. If you try to see me again I will report you to the elders." So saying she drove him from the house.

Nga Khwe reported back to his advisors, who bided their time until the next occasion when Than Than was left alone in the house. Then they plied him with strong drink and urged him to approach her again. "This time, don't accept any refusal" they counseled, "Take hold of her hand and embrace her even if she resists." Nga Khwe put a pen-knife in his pocket and left.

When he entered the house, he saw Than Than and immediately resumed telling her of his love. The girl was very indignant and berated him for his presumption. Nga Khwe stepped closer to her. "Don't you dare to come near me!" she warned, but he moved even closer and took her hand. Than Than tried to free herself, hurling curses at him all the while. Nga Khwe then drew the struggling girl into his arms, but she would not give in and continued screaming and slapping his face and fighting him off. Suddenly, there appeared in his mind the image of this girl smiling and welcoming her Chinese lover and unable to contain his jealousy any longer, he held her fast with his left arm, while he took out his knife and plunged it into her breast. He withdrew the blade and plunged it in again right up to the hilt. Than Than died in his arms. When Nga Khwe realised that she was dead, he found a deep pity for her welling up in his heart.

When the police came on the scene Nga Khwe left the house and ran into a sugar-cane shop. They followed and searched the premises for him, but he had burrowed himself under the discarded sugar-cane stalks and they could not find him. The proprietors knew where he was, but out of pity for him they did not reveal his hiding place to the policemen. Finally, he voluntarily rose from among the sugar cane to give himself up. In his hand he still held the murder weapon but was easily induced to part with it.

At his trial Nga Khwe made a full confession and was sentenced to ten years imprisonment. He was released at the end of 1955 from Rangoon Central Jail. His whereabouts are at present unknown.

II
IN THE RED LIGHT DISTRICT

I was born in a house near Ma Ohn Bridge in Kayan Town 19 years ago. My parents are U Ba Thin and Daw Chit Su. I have five brothers and sisters. Two brothers and two sisters are older than me and all four are already married. My younger brother still lives with my parents. Only one elder brother and one sister know how to read and write. The others are all illiterate.

When we lived in Kayan my parents supported us by rearing pigs. Originally we had three pigs and three cows, but before long they had increased to nearly thirty animals. However, this was not a very profitable business. Before the war my elder brothers and sisters stayed with my parents and helped them in their work.

Before the Japanese invaded Burma they bombed Kayan and we were nearly all killed. I had taken shelter under a nat-shrine when a bomb fell near it. In the confusion, our family was scattered, my father running one way, my mother another and the children being split into two groups. Finally, we children got together again in Laharywet village east of Kayan. My mother heard that my father had been seen in Rangoon and she followed him there. Only when she succeeded in tracing him did she write to us in Laharywet asking us to join them in Rangoon. The eldest brother decided to remain in the village. The second eldest brother carried my younger sister on his left shoulder and me on his right shoulder, while he led my elder sister by the hand and in this fashion we made our way to the capital. We were finally re-united with our parents near the Pazundaung foreshore. They had built a little hut there and there we stayed during the rest of the Japanese occupation.

Father supported us by hiring out as a water carrier. My brother took to drink and began to stay away from the house instead of helping father. Finally he left altogether to work as a bargee on a country boat. My father had a very difficult time trying to make both ends meet.

In spite of this he enrolled me when I was eight or nine in the Lower Pazundaung Alimoola Municipal School, now known as the Pyidawtha School. Within five years I had reached the fifth standard and I was studying Geography, Arithmetic, Burmese and English. By that time I had reached the age of fourteen. Around examination time I fell in love with a girl from the Fourth Standard named Apu who was about my age. One day she asked me to buy a pearl necklace for her and I did so. A boy named Mya Tin who was jealous of me went and told her mother who threatened to report me to the police. However, when they questioned the girl, they found that the necklace had been bought with her own money and she went on to confess that she was in love with me anyway. For this she was beaten soundly by her mother. Apu's mother had a lot of money, acquired through lending money at a monthly interest of ten percent and she considered me to be beneath her daughter. I felt humiliated at this and my friends made it worse by making fun of me. Between their taunts and my embarrassment, I lost all interest in my studies and left school.

I began working for some masons who were friendly with my father. As I was still a minor, I pretended to be grown up by wearing an old loin cloth as a turban. I was employed in the construction of the Government Technical Institute in front of the Royal Lakes in Rangoon at a daily wage of K 3.4 . Every morning I would leave for work at 6 a.m. carrying my lunch-box with me. Work began at 7 a.m. and went on till 4.30 p.m., with a one hour break for lunch at noon. If we worked overtime we were paid four annas an hour. In the evening, when I returned from work I would help my father to carry water for sale. We earned one anna per trip if the house we were supplying water to happened to be near to the water pump and two annas per trip if it were distant.

After seven or eight months of this work, my mother decided that the work was too strenuous for me and found another job for me stitching torn rice-sacks before they were loaded on to cargo boats. I also had to sweep the decks of the boats. The work was light compared to what I had been doing in my previous job, but I was paid only K 3/- a day, of which the foreman took a cut of 8 annas, leaving me only K 2.8 annas to take home. After a while my father stopped carrying water and joined me at my new place of employment on the boats. Between the two of us we began earning K 5/- a day.

When we had been working for two or three months, the foreman began to find fault with me. He did not like my occasional trips home to fetch lunch, or my habit of going and chatting with acquaintances on other parts of the vessel. I did not pay much heed to him when he berated me, until finally he lost all patience and fired me from the job.

When I got home my parents also scolded me and I felt miserable. Accordingly I consulted with four friends named Tin Aung, Myint Thein, Chit Sein and Pe Aung and we decided to run away to a place called Taungzun, taking with us whatever money we could scrape together. When we added this up, the total came up to about K 1000/-. The largest contribution was made by Tin Aung, whose parents owned a general provision store. My share was very little.

Tin Aung was unhappy because his parents had scolded him for failing the Eighth Standard Examination. Myint Thein had had to leave school to take a job as a trishawman, but he did not like the work as he felt it too tiring. Chit Sein was a former classmate of mine at Alimoola School whose parents were too poor to keep him in school and had entered him as an apprentice at a furniture shop. He was disheartened because he was not earning anything. Pe Aung had also left school in the Fifth Standard and found work at the Dawbon Dockyard cleaning engines and was dissatisfied with his low income.

We decided to go to a place called Taungzun because Chit Sein had his grandfather and other relatives there and because we had nowhere else to go. When we reached Taungzun we went to stay at the house of Chit Sein's grandfather U Sein and grandmother Daw Mya. During our stay there we did no work but spent the money we had brought with us in having a good time. We would follow schoolgirls and their teachers and young girls working at the cheroot making shop and inflict our unwelcome attentions on them. Soon their relatives became so incensed with us that they must have wanted to kill us.

About a month later, Tin Aung's uncle U Ba Khin and an elder from our neighbourhood named U Aung Bwint came to fetch us back to Rangoon. On the way home we had to spend a night at Sittaung. We wanted to visit a fair that was being held across the river, but we were not given permission. Accordingly we waited until the early hours of the morning when the elders were fast asleep and quietly stole out of the house with our baggage and ran away to a village called Nyaunkhashay. When the elders awoke and found us gone they telephoned from Sittaung to Nyaunkhashay and when we arrived at Nyaunkhashay station we were suddenly surrounded by policemen who levelled rifles at us and took us into custody.

The next train did not stop at Nyaunkhashay, but as it passed the station U Aung Bwint leaped off one of the carriages. He then approached us and hit Pe Aung in the face saying, "You already have a criminal case pending against you. Do you think you can run away like these others!" Pe Aung and a friend of his from the Dawbon Dockyard had quarrelled with workers from the Zaw Cinema and had been set upon and beaten up by them. Pe Aung had returned home to take an iron rod and had been searching for them when he was arrested by police. U Aung Bwint had provided bail for Pe Aung and had him released from the police lock-up, which was why he was so angry with the boy.

U Aung Bwint also turned to Tin Aung and saying "Your parents have been very good to you, why do you have to behave like this?", prepared to leave, taking Pe Aung and Tin Aung with him. He did not ask the rest of us to accompany him, perhaps fearing that he would not be able to control all five of us. However, I decided to go anyway.

We had to do the journey from Nyaungkhashay to Waw on foot. We left at noon and arrived only after nightfall. We could not find the headman since he was away at the wedding of his daughter to a rich man's son, so we went to the bus terminal and enquired after the bus that was to leave for Pegu in the morning. A passer-by pointed to a vehicle beside the road and said "That's the one over there." Accordingly we boarded the bus and spent the night on it.

In the morning we were surprised to find that there were no other passengers, nor did any driver or conductor appear. We got down from the bus and looked around, until one of us finally noticed that not only did our bus have no engine at all, but it had no gearbox or steering wheel as well. Only then did we realise that we had been victims of a practical joker. We thereupon boarded a bus whose conductor was shouting "Pegu, Pegu" and finally reached Pegu where we caught the train to Rangoon. We were ashamed because our whole neighbourhood had branded us as truants from home and so waited until nightfall before entering our houses. Once home, I resumed my previous life with my parents.

I could not find any other work, so I took to carrying water again for sale. Only after four months did I get a job at the Thanhmogyaink Rubber Works. At the end of three months I quarrelled with the foreman who threatened to beat me up and in disgust I ran away for the second time to Taungzun in the company of Chit Sein. For expenses we pawned the watch and ring which I had bought while working for the masons. After one month's stay in Taungzun, Chit Sein complained that he missed his mother, so giving him K 5-40 for train fare and K 6.00 for general expenses, I left for Moulmein.

I knew no one in Moulmein, but luckily I met an acquaintance from the Zaw Cinema who was working for Yadanabon Aye Maung's theatrical troupe in Daingwunkwin. I enlisted his help and he introduced me to the painter who illustrated posters and backdrop scenes for the show. This man hired me at K 3/- a day with meals on show nights and just meals with no pay on other nights. When the troupe moved away from Moulmein, he asked me to come along with him, but I declined and went back to Taungzun.

At Taungzun they were holding a festival in connection with a monk's cremation. Chit Sein's grandfather U Sein had set up a gambling booth and I helped him to run it. While there I met a girl called Kyi Khin and we fell in love. I asked her to run away with me to Rangoon, but she demurred, saying that she knew of several cases where village girls had trusted their sweethearts from Rangoon and accompanied them to the city, only to come to grief in a very short time. She said I should approach her parents formally and ask for her hand in marriage. I promised her that I would do so in two months time, during which I would return to Rangoon and save up some money.

Upon arriving in Rangoon I found that the painter Ko Tin U had preceeded me there. He had set up a studio in front of Zaw Cinema, and I went to work for him as an assistant.

The neighbourhood in which I stayed is called Alimoola, and is continuous with the notorious Alimoola locality of which you have doubtless heard. One day, while a friend named Nyunt Tin and I were decorating a tree with religious offerings, a girl from a nearby house called out to me and asked me if I had some matches. I went over and handed her a box, when she caught hold of my hands and kissed me. "What on earth are you doing! Have a care. People will see us." I said to her in embarrassment, but she declared "Let them see us. I love you and I don't care who knows it."

This girl's name was Ma Khin Myint and she was a few years older than me. She had come to Rangoon from Bogale. In about a week's time we had become man and wife.

In her house were three other girls living with her who were of the same age as Ma Khin Myint. There was also a married woman about thirty years old named Atint whom the girls called "mother". The girls were all eighteen or nineteen. Every morning they would bathe and put on new clothes and make up their faces and put flowers in their hair and generally make themselves beautiful. They would then sit down and wait. I would usually leave the house early, drop in at the corner tea-shop, visit friends, take meals at my mother's place and return home only at night. Within three or four days I began to grow suspicious at the stream of visitors coming to the house. One day, on coming home in the evening I saw my wife emerging from the bedroom with a huge Indian. That night I taxed her with it and she confessed to me that she was a prostitute. I pleaded with her to give up this occupation and move with me to my mother's house, but Atint whispered something to her and Ma Khin Myint informed me that she preferred to stay where she was. Accordingly I left her and came away. We were married only for about eight days.

Actually Ma Khin Myint refused to accompany me, not because she was enamoured of the life nor for lack of love for me, but because she was afraid of the pimp, Atint's husband. Three days later, Ma Khin Myint ran away from the house, but not knowing her way around town, was caught and beaten by Atint and her husband. Before long she ran away again and this time was apprehended by the police. When she told the police that she had run away from a brothel they gave her into the custody of an elder from the Alimoola ward. This man straight-away returned her to Atint's house and there she had to stay until she eventually fell in love with a trishawman living nearby and moved into his house. Since this man was an upright fellow earning a living by honest means and had legally taken her as his wife Atint and her husband did not dare to interfere any longer and left her in peace.

Ma Khin Myint's entry into the profession followed the usual pattern. A well dressed young man from Rangoon had come to Bogale and courted her, after which he had asked her parents for her hand in marraige and taken her to Rangoon. Once there she was forced to become a prostitute. After a while she was sold to another brothel for three or four hundred kyats. The friends who originally ran away to Taungzun with me were a bad lot. Myint Thein married Atint the wife of Ma Khin Myint's pimp and made her work as a prostitute for him. Chit Sein stole her away from Myint Thein. Chit Sein was a favourite with the girls. He had a nice singing voice and could melt the heart of any girl until she was ready to do anything for him.

After some time Chit Sein asked me to accompany Atint to Moulmein, her place of birth, saying that he would follow us in a short while. However, he failed to appear in Moulmein and while waiting for him we began having sexual relations. Atint kept pining for him, telling people that she and I were just friends and that her husband would be coming soon. In the meantime she supported me by vending fish.

For a whole month I did no work, but after that I tried my hand at pedalling a trishaw. However, I was not strong enough for the job and the hilly roads of Moulmein did not make things easier for me. I managed to earn only about seventy-five pyas a day, so after three days I gave up. I tried to convince Atint that we should go back to Rangoon, but she could not be persuaded to leave her sisters. We both knew that her sisters were arranging to have her married to an Indian trader.

I returned to the city alone. Five days later Atint appeared in Rangoon. When she met Chit Sein, she upbraided him for not keeping to his promise, but he explained that he had been unable to join her in the village because he did not have the passage money. At the same time he refused to take her back. Finally she went back to live with Myint Thein.

One day feeling downcast because I had no money I made a day trip to Pegu. On the train I noticed a woman with a valuable necklace around her neck. As the train pulled out of Dahbein Station I laid hold of the necklace and jumped off. Unfortunately, the rope was too strong and securely fastened and did not break. The woman shouted for help and I was seized by a crowd.

At the police station I protested that I had been wrongfully arrested and that I had jumped off the train merely to get a drink of water, but nobody believed me and I was sent up for trial before the Hlegu magistrate. At the trial the plaintiff did not appear but I was found guilty anyway and fined ten kyats. As I did not have the money to pay the fine, I was sentenced to six month's imprisonment. I was just sixteen years old at that time.

When I was released from prison I no longer dared to go home to my parents. I went to live at the house of Ko Than on the Alimoola foreshore with my friend Nyunt Tin who had run away from home. The ward elders hired the two of us as watchmen. Our job was to keep a lookout for fires, thieves and bandits, and we were each paid one kyat and fifty pyas per night. The pay was meagre, but we supplemented it by holding up people who came to the neighbourhood to look for prostitutes. We did not take all they had, only three kyats to five kyats from each person. Sometimes we would lead them on saying that we could take them to the brothels and only when they had entered the premises would we rob them. Since they themselves were breaking the law, none of our victims ever reported us to the police.

After about three months Nyunt Tin's parents came for him and placed him in a job on a ship. I moved in with a pimp named Kala and his brother Ba Myint. At first I did no work for Kala but rolled about in a deck chair all day.

Kala's wife Ma Thein Nyunt was one of the prostitutes. There were two other girls who were also working for him. The income was very good but Kala spent it all at the racecourse and at gambling houses.

Later, Kala tried to use me to decoy young innocent girls to his brothel. I was to court them and become their lover, after which I was to turn them over to him for service in his house. Kala sent me on these missions to various places like Kyaukmyaung and Danyingon. At first I found no success whatsoever. Then one day I met an eighteen year old girl who was working as a maid in a house near the Tamwe traffic circle. She was feeling downhearted because there were no opportunities for advancement in her job, and readily consented to come along with me. When we arrived at Kala's house he gave me some money and sent me off along to the cinema. That night according to the etiquette governing such matters, Kala invited fifteen other brothel keepers to his house and they all had sexual relations with her that night, Kala beating her into submission every time she tried to fight someone off.

The following morning she was forced to begin accepting regular cash-paying customers. The girl protested tearfully that she did not want to do this work, saying that she had come along only because she loved me and demanded to know where I was. They told her that I had sold her to the brothel and that she would never set eyes on me again. When she started to cry anew, Kala's wife and the other prostitutes consoled her saying "Why don't you give in? You can have a wonderful time here. We will buy you jewelry and beautiful clothes and anything else that you fancy. And anyway, what difference does it make now? It is too late to change anything, so you might as well get something out of it." Then they wiped away her tears and made much of her, brewing tea for her to drink and making her up so as to look pretty. When the next customer came and she was summoned she again refused to submit, declaring "I am a good girl of respectable parents and I cannot do this sort of work. Please bring Ko Kyaw Tha to me," whereupon Kala gave her another beating, after which the prostitutes consoled her again and resumed their blandishments.

The favours of a new arrival could be obtained on a payment of ten kyats but regular customers were charged only three to five kyats. The young maid alone fetched over one hundred kyats in a single night. Only after two or three days was I permitted to re-enter the house. This was done so as to reconcile the girl to her lot. When she saw me she threw herself into my arms, crying "Where have you been?" and wept. Kala and his brother locked us up in a bedroom where I was supposed to spent the night with her. I tried my best to comfort her and gradually her tears lessened and finally ceased.

When she related all that had happened to her during my absence, I felt extremely sorry for her and bitterly regretted my part in the affair. I therefore determined to rescue her if I could. The room was locked from the outside and the key kept under Kala's pillow. I listened intently and realizing that the whole house was asleep I quietly climbed over the partition, stealthily extracted the key from under Kala's pillow and opening the front door, told the girl to flee.

After she had gone I was consumed with anxiety for her sake, because there was an understanding on the part of all brothels that a reward of fifty kyats would be paid to anyone who caught and returned an absconder. If she were apprehended my situation would also be extremely perilous.

I was so worried that I could not sleep at all that night. At four p.m. I woke up Kala and Nyunt Yin and informed them that the girl was missing. They examined the key hanging from the lock and searched the house and grounds. Kala sent me out to scour the neighbourhood, saying that she did not know her way and was bound to be wandering around. I went out and pretended to look for her, returning in the morning to report that my mission had been unsuccessful. Kala took the news philosophically. "Well, that can't be helped," he said, "we shall have to find another girl to take her place. But it is a pity that this one got away."

The brothel-keepers in the neighbourhood hated me but the prostitutes were all fond of me. This was because I was always kind to them and felt friendly towards them. Once, while I was standing on a corner, a young prostitute named Thein Kyi ran up to me and seizing me by the arm cried breathlessly "Oh! please save me! I am running away." I said nothing but gently disengaged her fingers from my arm and pointed down one street. A few minutes after she had disappeared a group of five men came running up to me and said "Did you see a young girl running past? Show us the way she went and you will get fifty kyats." "Yes!" I replied, "I saw her all right. She went that way." and pointed to a different street from the one she had taken. They went off immediately in this wrong direction and needless to say failed to catch up with her and she escaped. The pimps later came to suspect that I had given them a wrong lead and became very annoyed with me.

At one time when the police were raiding houses over the entire Alimoola neighbourhood in a clean-up drive, all the brothels closed their doors and the prostitutes temporarily moved elsewhere to stay out of their way. One day while we were visiting the Sule Pagoda I came upon the young maid from Tamwe selling flowers on the precincts of the Pagoda. I greeted her and quickly said "Those fellows are with me". Kala and Tin Nyunt were some little distance away and did not see her. As soon as she heard that they were around, she got up intending to go and assault them with her slipper, but I restrained her, pointing out that they would very likely find some means of forcing her back to the brothel. She realised the truth of this and ran off to hide in a safe place until we were gone.

During this period the inmates of the Alimoola brothels spent all their afternoons visiting various pagodas such as Botataung, Sule, Shwedagon, Kaba Aye, Ngatatkyi, Chauktatgyi and other places such as the Royal Lakes and the Zoo. One day I happened to mention that I had met the Tamwe girl at Sule Pagoda. Kala immediately told me to go and fetch her, saying that she would boost our earnings quite a bit, but I demurred, pointing out that she had been a chance visitor who had come to pray at the pagoda and therefore impossible to trace.

Kala's income was considerable, his daily take being anywhere from fifty to a hundred kyats. However, he would lose most of it in gambling and his wife Nyunt Yin had to then pawn her jewelry to provide him with another stake. To add to her misery he would blame her when there were not enough customers. Partly because he could not spare the time to bring in fresh customers and partly due to the fact that he would pawn their jewelry to cover his gambling losses, the other two girls in the house ran away and Nyunt Yin was left alone to support Kala with her earnings. His income fell to between thirty and fifty kyats a day. This was too little to suit Kala and he began to berate her for it. After a while Nyunt Yin could stand it no longer and decided to escape. She tried to get me to accompany her. Knowing her story I felt very sympathetic to her, but I was afraid of what Kala might do to me, so taking her to the Insein Bus Stand I put her on a bus and returned to Kala's house pretending that I had no hand in the matter.

Nyunt Yin's story was a familiar one. She formerly lived in Insein No 8 Compound with her family. Her father was a foreman. When he died the family had to give up their quarters and move into the village. To help out, Nyunt Yin who was growing into adolescence, had to go round town selling treacle rice. One day a pimp named Ngawetkalay saw her at Myenigon and deciding that she was ripe for the plucking, managed to induce her to take up prostitution to supplement her meagre earnings. From that time on Nyunt Yin would come everyday to Myenigon with her basket of treacle rice and leave only in the evening. Her mother and brother had no inkling of her activities.

Ngawetkalay and his brother Nyipulay were from Pegu. They had been working as manual labourers, but when Nyunt Yin fell into their hands they realised that they had been given a golden opportunity to attain a life of ease and plenty. They brought her to Alimoola and set up a brothel there. Nyunt Yin was no longer permitted to return home in the evenings. All her earnings were appropriated by Ngawetkalay and if they did not seem sufficient she was beaten.

She did not receive money for herself and so could not send any to her mother. She grew unhappy and one day when she saw me at the Nyaungdan Jetty she appealed to me for help. I took her to the Theingyizay Bus Stand and put her on an Insein Bus that would carry her home.

Since they had been living as man and wife, Ngawetkalay boldly followed her to her village and pleaded with her to come back. Nyunt Yin had not dared to tell her mother and her brother, one of whom was a sergeant in the Army, of the life she had been leading and so was persuaded by them to return to Rangoon with her husband.

One day while Ngawetkalay was out gambling, Nyunt Yin was approached by Kala, who declared that he loved her and induced her to run away to Syriam with him. At Syriam Kala worked as a trishawman, while he made Nyunt Yin resume working as a prostitute. Ngawetkalay did not follow them to Syriam. About three months later Kala brought back Nyunt Yin to Alimoola and installed her in a brothel and it was there that I met them.

When Nyunt Yin's absence was discovered I was interrogated by Kala, Hla Myint, Aung Baw and Hoke Gwan. I denied that I had helped her to escape and told them that I would have informed them if I had known of her plans. They did not believe me and were very angry with me. They had been drinking and one of them seized a bottle by the neck to hit me with but I stepped back and picked up an iron poker. I was outnumbered four to one, but they were half drunk and no match for me, so they calmed down. The next day they continued their search for the missing girl and towards evening they located her in the house of her aunt in Insein and brought her back.

When we had a moment alone Nyunt Yin upbraided me. "You lied to me. You promised that you would follow me, but did not come." "I did not have the fare", I replied, "And besides, Kala was watching me too closely."

Nyunt Yin's situation was not improved in any way upon her return. As before she had to turn over all her earnings to Kala who spent it all at the gambling tables and her jewelry had to be pawned again. She determined to run away again and sought my advice. "This time if you go, try and make a clean get-a-way." I told her. She urged me to come along with her. She also wanted to save up some money and redeem her valuables before leaving, but I counselled her to go at once, pointing out that if she were to remain attached to her jewels she would not be able to make a clean break with this sort of life. She was finally convinced and we made plans to run away together.

On the appointed day we had arranged to meet at the Insein Bus Stand, but there was a hitch and at five in the evening Nyunt Yin crossed the river to Syriam. This time for some reason Kala did not scold me, but sent me and Hoke Gwan to search for her. We visited many places and I made a great show of looking for her. I had decided that if we should accidently come upon Nyunt Yin, I would assault Hoke Gwan and make my escape with her. Luckily, the contingency did not arise. After a while it began to rain heavily and we became soaked to the skin. When we returned home we had no change of clothes, because they were all at the pawn-shop, so we wrapped blankets around ourselves and hung up our clothes to dry. Kala was dissatisfied at our failure. "This girl does not know how to go anywhere" he declared angrily. "She must be hiding somewhere nearby," and went out to look for her. He also made us resume the search. But she was nowhere to be found.

Early the next morning Nyunt Yin crossed the river again in a sampan. At about seven a.m. she arrived at the Pazundaung Nyaungdan Jetty, where I was playing marbles with a boy called Tin Tun. She called out to me softly and when I ran up to her she quickly bundled me onto the boat and we rowed off towards Dawbon. When Tin Tun was out of sight however we turned around and rowed back towards Pazundaung Bazaar. Our caution proved to be justified because word got back immediately to Kala through Tin Tun that I had gone away in a sampan to Dawbon with the missing girl. Kala and his friends at once seized long swords and rushed to Dawbon to wait for our arrival, but by that time we were on the bus to Insein. I had resolved that if they followed us and tried to board the bus I would kick them off. It would be better however, if they did not find us at all, so we took care to cover our faces and chose the corner seats on the bus, so as not to be seen from outside. As we had anticipated, a jeep containing Kala and his group overtook the bus and sometime later passed us on its way back. Our presence on the bus went undetected.

Upon arriving at Insein we went to the Hlaing River near Bawseik, and sat down on the bank. A man carrying paddy called out to me, "Where are you from? Are you an Army deserter?" I replied that I was no deserter, but that we had eloped, and were sitting there because we did not know what to do and had no place to go.

The friendly workman immediately invited us to come and stay with him. We accepted gratefully and spent about ten days in his house. By the end of that period the fifty kyats that we had between us was almost gone and we discussed what we should do. Nyunt Yin suggested that we should go and stay with her mother at Ywama. We would work at whatever job we could get. Having no better alternative to offer I agreed.

Nyunt Yin's mother was overjoyed at her daugther's return, and built us a small hut adjacent to her own. She also told us to ask her for whatever money we needed to tide us over the period before we were again employed.

Fifteen days after our arrival at Ywama, Kala, Hoke Guan, Hla Thaung and two others appeared in a jeep. Instead of driving up to the house they waited at the edge of the jungle. When they saw Nyunt Yin's young cousin they approached her and gave her a ring, telling her to go and call me and Nyunt Yin as they had some matters to discuss with us. They said that they had found work for us at a mason's. We were still out of work at this time and they must have been well aware of it. Nyunt Yin's mother refused to let me go, and sent Nyunt Yin and her younger sister and brothers instead. A little while after they had gone, I grew worried and followed them.

When I reached the edge of the clearing Kala and the others were chasing Nyunt Yin. Hla Thaung came running towards me. I picked up a clod of earth and shouted: "Stand back!" Kala called out to me that he had already reported to me at the police station for having eloped with his wife. Nyunt Yin ran into her mother's house and he went in after her. I took up a position in a nearby house and listened.

"I cannot stand being separated from my wife. That young fellow stole her away from me," Kala was saying to Nyunt Yin's mother. Nyunt Yin on her part heatedly began to relate everything that had happened to her at Kala place, whereupon Nyunt Yin's relatives became enraged and were about to attack him, when I intervened and managed to calm them down.

Kala kept repeating that he could not give up Nyunt Yin. If she did not want to live with him, he was willing to accept that and she could remain with her mother. But she would still be his wife, and he would send her money for her maintenance. However, if she insisted on living with me as my wife, he would see to it that I went to jail and then he would force Nyunt Yin to return to him.

While all this was going on, Hla Thaung had rushed to my house to fetch my mother, and now my mother and brother-in-law arrived on the scene. After listening to the story, they began entreating me to come back with them and leave Nyunt Yin with her mother. I refused, but after much persuasion I had to give in. We went back to Rangoon in Kala's jeep, after a stern warning was given to Kala by the villagers not to touch a hair of my head.

When we reached East Rangoon Kala ordered the driver to drive to the police station, saying that he was going to deliver me into police custody. I told him to go ahead, that I was ready to tell the police everything about his activities, and that Nyunt Yin would also testify that he had made her work as a prostitute for him. This made him change his mind, and he told the driver to drive to Alimoola instead.

At that time Alimoola was notorious as a red-light district, boasting of more than sixty brothels, complete with brothel keepers, pimps, prostitutes, and their hangers-on. Some policemen were levying money on the brothels, raiding houses which refused to pay and giving advance warning of impending raids to the others. As soon as word arrived that a raid was imminent the girls would run outside and sit down in the roadside stalls, pretending to be selling mangoes and vegetables. Other would take refuge in neighbouring houses, whose householders would protect them from the police, comfirming that the girls were indeed relatives of theirs.

In a brothel the prostitutes have to rise early bathe and dress up in attractive clothes, make themselves pretty and assume a cheerful demeanor. On no account were they allowed to look glum or sulky, or to quarrel among themselves. Such behaviour was likely to drive away customers and was generally punished with severe beatings. Discipline was strict, the girls went in fear and trembling of the brothel keeper and his wife.

A popular girl could entertain as many as fifty men in a day, and great care was taken to see that such good earners were not incapacitated by pregnancy or disease. In case of infection a medical practioner was called in. This man was not a qualified doctor and had no license to practice. He was paid five kyats for a visit, and five kyats for each penicillin injection he administered. In spite of this many girls contracted venereal diseases. A girl named Akyaing has even become a leper.

The first signs of disease are the small swellings on the face somewhat skin to mosquito bites. They itch terribly, but when you scratch them, they turn septic and pus begins to form. If you scratch them further, the sores become larger and the fingers begin to contract. Should such a person eat foods such as beef or chicken her condition rapidly worsens.

In a short while the patient is no longer able to hold a spoon in her fingers. Nor does she dare to show her face outside. She goes to her grave in this condition.

Brothel keepers sternly forbid the eating of chicken and beef in their houses, but the prostitutes break their rule whenever possible. Trying to prevent them from eating such meat merely whets their appetites all the more. Of course, they need all the energy they can get from the food they eat. The work they engage in is very strenuous, especially round about the first of the month, when office workers and soldiers draw their salaries.

Some of the girls became pregnant and gave birth to babies that were either deformed, or were syphilitic. The mother cherished these babies and lavished all their love and attention on them.

In the neighbourhood, boys of nine or ten would play truant from school and engage in drumming up customers for the brothels. When well-meaing individuals scolded them for not going to school, they would retort that they were earning good money this way while they would get nothing by attending school. Some parents would berate their children for such activities but others welcomed them as supplementing an uncertain family income. The children of course would not turn over their entire earnings, but keep a portion of the money for themselves, to pay for cinema tickets, sweets and cigarettes.

These boys were adept at their work. Whenever a likely look-ing prospect appeared they would run along beside him, saying: "Do you want a girl? We can take you to some pretty ones." and so on. If a policeman came along they would immediately dive into the stream nearby and pretend to be swimming and playing, only to emerge as soon as he departed to carry on where they had left off.

When the children delivered a customer to a brothel they were given between fifteen to twenty percent of the fee. If they were unfortunate, they would meet a pimp on the way to the brothel, in which case he would chase them away with threats and blows and deliver the customer to the brothel himself. Trishawmen also received a commission for the trade they brought in.

Whenever a stranger passed through the quarter the air would re-sound with the cries of the prostitutes calling out to him and inviting him to enter. "Come on up!" they would call "where are you off to? Where else can you find a girl as pretty as me?" and so on. All this could be most embarassing to a man who had unwittingly entered the area. If the man happened to be an Indian they would speak in Hindi. Competition between the prostitutes was fierce, because each brothel keeper would tote up the takings at the end of the day and if he was dissatisfied with the daily earnings he would rail at the girls and quite often beat them.

One day a wandering astrologer came up our street and a girl from our house called out an invitation to him. The old man was hard of hearing, but entered immediately and taking a seat on the mat produced his slate and slate-pencil and asked the girl "What is your date of birth?" We looked at one another and burst into laughter. Finally someone said to him "This girl didn't call you to have her for-tune told, but to ask you if you wanted to have some fun with her." At that the old man became flustered saying "No, No, I know nothing of such matters," beat a hasty retreat, leaving behind his slate and pencil in his confusion.

At pagoda festivals and other fairs where crowds foregathered, the brothel keepers would keep a sharp lookout for young girls who may have become separated from their parents or elders. When one of them spotted such a girl they would approach her and offer to take her back to her chaperone. If she believed him and followed him, he would bring her directly to the brothel. After keeping the girl in his house for four or five days he would sell her to another brothel keeper, telling her to go along with the man as he would take her back home.

A beautiful girl with a good figure would fetch as much as five hundred kyats. Others were sold for three to four hundred kyats. They even had appraisers to determine the value of each girl. Whenever a new girl arrived in the Alimoola ward, her owner had to invite about fifteen other brothel keepers to sleep with the girl on the first night. Only after that was she made available to the general public.

The police were well aware of all that was going on and just before the convening of the Sixth Great Buddhist Synod to commemorate the 2500th anniversary of the advent of Buddhism, they rounded up all the proprietors of the major brothels. However, the lesser known brothels continued their operations unchecked.

In the neighbourhood there was a household where a man lived with his young son, his two daughters and their husbands. One of the husbands was a trishawman and the other was a member of the Armed Services. Both the girls were working as prostitutes in that very house. The husbands were well aware of this and may have been a-betting them in their activities. At any rate they did not make any protest. The father too knew what was going on. Worst of all, the young brother was working as a pimp for his sisters.

I have related my story and all I know about the prostitution business without holding anything back in the hope that it may help some of the girls to escape this racket and to enable other young boys to obtain a better chance than I received. I am running a great danger in telling you all this, but that cannot be helped. And from what I hear, the police have been cracking down on the Alimoola brothels. The prostitutes and their pimps and brothel keepers have fled to other localities. Many of them, including Kala and Nyunt Yin have moved to Mandalay. This news was given to me by someone from Alimoola who entered the prison about three months after I did.

My imprisonment had nothing to do with prostitution. A friend named Hmat-Gyi asked me to take him on a trishaw to a certain place where he wanted to steal a motor-battery from the bus. After a while there was a hue and cry, Hmat Gyi came running past and threw the battery down near the trishaw as he went by. Finding the battery near me the crowd set upon me. To give Hmat Gyi time to escape, I fought back, but then somebody hit me from behind I lost consciousness. When I came to, I found myself in the Pazundaung Lock-up.

Hmat Gyi was apprehended but because of his youth was given bail. I was sent here and have been here since June 1956. Hearing on my case has been deferred eight times because the plaintiff did not appear. My parents are too poor to hire a lawyer for me. The other day I took my courage in my hands and requested the judge to dispose of my case soon and he promised to do so.

*

Maung Kyaw Tha was released from prison in October 1956. Whether he was acquitted or had been merely granted bail I was unable to determine. When the author was set free in October 1957 Maung Kyaw Tha had still not returned to the prison.

III
SLEIGHT OF HAND

My name is Johnny Jijina and I was born in Shanghai, China. My father was Peter Jijina. My mother's name is Jennie Jijina. They were originally from Iran. When they first arrived in Shanghai my parents were extremely poor and with the coming of the Japanese things became even more difficult for them. Movement of all goods was prohibited by the Japanese and any infraction of this law was punishable by death. My father made a living by transporting rice and opium from Shanghai to cities such as Shugyo, Chinkiang, Muhsi, Nanking and their outlying villages.

Father spoke Chinese but not as fluently as I could. I could speak Chinese very well, having grown up together with children of Chinese neighbours. My father accordingly took me with him on his trips.

In Shanghai we lived in the French sector. Since there were many White Russians living there we learned to speak Russian as well.

The Japanese had interned all the English and Americans. The Persians were given red arm bands to wear. When visiting other towns and villages these arm bands had to be removed.

On our trips we pretended to be White Russians. At that time there was a sizable White Russian population in Shanghai. These were Russians who had fled their country after the Russian Revolution of 1919. They did not seem to have any patriotic feelings, but spent their time in drinking and playing and generally having a good time. They were perpetually hard up and would sell anything they had, even the identity cards which the Japanese had issued to them. These identity cards were then altered to show the picture of the new owner and doctored so as to be indistinguishable from the original.

Some White Russians enlisted in the Japanese army and others served as armed guards at railway stations. The Japanese placed a great deal of trust in them and so it was a wise move on our part to pretend that we were White Russians. The fact that we both spoke Russian made it unlikely that our impersonation would be discovered.

To carry a heavy commodity like rice we had to hire three coolies. We would make inquiries in advance and take the route that was free of Japanese road blocks and search parties, often walking twelve or thirteen miles a day.

I was eight years old at the time. I could not speak Japanese but my parents and sisters could all speak it quite well. The Japanese did not consider us enemies and consequently did not give us any trouble. However, my sisters were growing up and my parents were worried on their account.

On one occasion my sisters accompanied us on a trip to another town. We put up for the night in a small hotel. That night five drunken Japanese soldiers turned up and asked for the loan of my sisters. My father remonstrated with them but they kept demanding that the girls come along with them. Finally they tried to use force but one of my sisters managed to escape from the hotel. She ran to the Japanese Kempetai Military Police to report the matter to them. The Kempetai came at once and took away the drunken soldiers.

In 1945 when the American troops occupied Shanghai, my father opened a hotel. My two sisters were very pretty and could dance very well and their presence made the hotel very popular. Since there was drinks, dancing and food available on the premises, the hotel made a lot of money.

At that time I was about twelve years old. My mother gave me pocket money but I found it quite insufficient. I had a lot of friends of various nationalities, and we would spend our time in drinking, seeing shows and in roaming around. In our group were boys who could steal and pickpocket, and the rest of us soon learnt their arts from them. I became very proficient at making objects disappear from my hand. This was the beginning of my downfall.

When I reached the age of seventeen, I married Mary Mehalyi, a girl who was living with my mother. Mary was a Persian like us. She was fifteen at the time. I did not have any steady job, my work consisting solely of filching goods from shops.

When the communists took over in 1949, the hotel business

declined. People no longer patronised restaurants featuring drinks and dancing. Most of our patrons, the Europeans and other whites left the country and my parents therefore decided to leave as well. We made our way to the Burma border by way of Kwan-gyo, Hin-yan, Kwan-min and Wan-tin on motor trucks. When we arrived in Lashio the Burmese government took care of us. We stayed in Lashio for one and a half months and then moved to Maymyo, where we stayed for another two months. While in Maymyo we put on a variety show that ran for five days.

The Burmese government gave us quarters near the railway station in Mandalay. We were also given money but this was far too little for our needs. There were thirty people in our group which comprised thirteen adult males, eleven adult females and twelve children. Of this group some have returned to Iran, many have moved to India and only a few now remain in Burma.

There were fifteen and sixteen year old girls in our group and they were subjected to a great deal of teasing on the part of the young men in the neighbourhood. These men would waylay the girls when they were sent out to buy tea and proposition them. An Anglo-Indian boy named Robertson who worked in the Burma Railways fell in love with one of the girls called Jennie Guranuna and followed her to Mandalay when we moved there. About six months later, just on the eve of our departure for Rangoon they eloped. Her mother was distraught because arrangements had already been made for their family to embark for Iran after a short stay in Rangoon but the couple were nowhere to be found, and finally we had to leave them behind.

We arrived in Rangoon in August 1950. We were given accomodation in Thingangyun, but they were far smaller than what we required. A few police constables under an inspector of police were detailed to guard us. We put on a show at the Green Hotel in Rangoon and made a lot of money from it but this did not last very long and as we were not permitted to do other work outside, it became increasingly difficult for us to make both ends meet. Accordingly, we requested permission to visit the city and our request was granted. Three of us left in the charge of a police constable. When we arrived in town we at once made for the Rangoon Restaurant on Sule Pagoda Road and left the constable there with one of our number with instructions that the policeman be plied with food and drink at our expense.

Meanwhile, we made the best use of our time by visiting the various shops and restaurants in town, picking pockets and pilfering from shops. We were back within an hour or two in time to make the five o'clock deadline set for us by the authorities. We made several such trips into Rangoon until the authorities finally got wind of the matter. However, they knew that we were not engaged in spying, so they took no action against us. Soon after this we were all granted permission to move out of the camps and stay where we liked provided we kept the authorities informed of our whereabouts. Our family found accomodation near the Mayoson Cinema on Kyaikasan Road in Tamwe. By this time we were paying our own rent.

My elder brother had left for India with my two sisters, leaving only my parents, my wife and I and our child in Burma. My father had grown too old to work any more and I had become the sole breadwinner in the family. I managed to find employment as a chauffer in a house near the Indian Embassy at 120 kyats a month. This was insufficient to meet the needs of our family and so whenever I had any spare time I would go out and try to augment my earnings by pickpocketing or shoplifting or cheating.

After about a year of this I was arrested and sent to prison for the first time. My father died while I was being held in the lockup prior to the passing of sentence. In her letters to me my mother made no mention of his death. After fifteen days I was sentenced to either 6 months imprisonment or 20 lashes. I chose the lashes and returned home to find that my father had died and that there was no food in the house.

I had lost my job as a chauffeur nor could I get any other work, so I reverted to my old ways. A year later my wife gave birth to another daughter. When the baby was two months old I took a trip to Pyapon in the company of a Pathan named Mohamed Raju and we were arrested and I was sentenced to one year's imprisonment in Pyapon jail. However, owing to the remissions of sentence which we were granted for the Pegu Shwemawdaw Pagoda Festival and the festival celebrating the opening of the Sixth Great Buddhist Synod I was released from prison after serving only five months.

While I was in prison my wife had managed to get a job as a dance instructress at a dancing school on 40th Street. She was given free lodging and a salary of one hundred kyats a month. Since my name and my photograph had been printed in the newspaper accounts of the Pyapon affair, I found it absolutely impossible to get any job. I did not wish to live on my wife's earnings, which were very meagre anyway and so turned once again to the only means of gaining money left to me.

Fearing that I had become too well known in Rangoon to avoid detection for long, I took to making trips to the outlying districts. In this way I visited Myaungmya, Bassein, Kyaiklat, Bogale, Moulmeingyun, Wakema, in the Irrawaddy Delta, as well as most towns in Upper Burma, including Taungyi, Kalaw, Lashio, Meiktila, Mandalay, Sagaing, Shwebo and even a small town called Kyonkadoo. Occasionally my wife would accompany me on these trips, leaving the children with my mother. The only towns we did not visit were those in the Arakan and Tennasserim Divisions.

By this time we could speak Burmese quite fluently. We took with us penicillin and other medicines pretending that we were dealing in these goods. Whenever we arrived at a town, we would go to a restaurant and order a meal there. If we had not been able to find a better place to sleep we would ask the proprietor for permission to stay the night, offering to pay for our lodging. We were rarely turned away and some would even refuse to take any money but we made it a point to insist on paying them.

You may have read the account of our arrest in Mandalay. My wife was also arrested together with me. I pleaded with the police station officer begging him to let us go and promising to leave town the very next day if he did so. The officer seems to have been moved by my appeal and in turn managed to persuade the complainant to drop the case.

As soon as we were released from custody we hired a taxi jeep to take us to Maymyo where we registered at the Strand Hotel. In Maymyo we did not make much money so we moved on to Lashio, where we managed to get K 220/- and a few pieces of gold. Returning to Mandalay, we went on to Shwebo where we picked up K 300/-. From Shwebo we took a jeep to Loilem where we stole K 350/- and a wrist watch. We stayed in Taungyi for one night. The next day we hired a jeep for K 125/- for a trip to Meiktila. Asking the driver to hold it in readiness we went to a shop selling monks' apparel and other requisites and on the pretense of changing some money, managed to get away with K 1200/-. After a hurried trip to Meiktila, we returned to Rangoon the next day via Thazi.

We arrived in Rangoon just in time to attend the hearings on a case involving both me and a man named Baldwin. Baldwin was not a Persian. He was either a Jew or an Anglo-Indian. The two of us had managed to lift the wallet of a Sub-Divisional Police Officer. We were not caught then, but evidently he must have suspected us, for sometime later, when he met us on Kokine Road he stopped and searched us. Finding K 60/- in our pockets, he declared that K 40/- of it was his money and arrested us. The Honorary Magistrate sentenced both of us to one year's imprisonment and I entered this prison on 8-7-55.

If I could find a worthwhile job I would try and lead an honest life. If possible I would like to go to India, where my brothers and sisters and my brother-in-law have already gone. I have decided to try and stay out of prison because of the difficulties which my family have to face whenever I am jailed. But I do not know whether this will be possible.

The other day I received a letter from my mother in which she gave me some news about Jennie Guranuna. Robertson had taken Jennie with him to England, where because of her good looks she became very popular. Robertson became very jealous at Jennie's going out with other men and one day he poisoned her. Robertson's sister had reported the matter to the police and he was now in custody. I hope and pray that this piece of news is false, because if it were true it would be a sorry business indeed.

*

Johnny Jijina is a slim man about six feet tall and about twenty-three years of age. His features are somewhat Semitic and he is often mistaken for a Jew. He has a winning manner and considerable force of personality. His hands are huge and this must have been of great assistance to him in his chosen profession. In the prison he gave a most convincing demonstration of how easy it was, armed with just a pair of scissors, to transform some old newspapers into what appeared to be a packet of currency notes.

After relating his story to me Johnny Jijina was imprisoned twice. By this time he had become embarrassed to see me and would not consent to meet me again and so I could not find out the reasons for his return to the jail.

IV
MURDER IN THE FIELDS

My name is *Lay* not *Mr. Lay*. I am a true Mon. I think I must be about 28 years old. I am from Kamarwet village, Mudon Township, Moulmein District. My father's name is U Hinn and my mother's name is Ma Sein Htun. My parents earned their living as farmers, working about 35 acres of land. They owned five pairs of draught oxen. I have one elder brother, one younger sister and one younger brother. They are at present still living in our village together with my parents.

I studied in Primary School for only three months and in a Buddhist monastic school for about a year. After that I had to help my parents in the fields.

I can read Burmese quite well now. When this jail became a Model Prison they started a school here and I enrolled for classes. I can now write a little and can read quite fluently. I can read newspapers and understand what I read.

Most of the people in our village are farmers. There are also a few who work in the rubber plantations. There are about one thousand households in the village which is administered by four headmen. The two Government recognized schools in the village teach both the Burmese and Mon languages. The village is situated near the highway to Kyaikkhami Town and is about six miles from Mudon.

My trouble began when I got into the wrong company.

During the paddy reaping season I was asleep in the field hut one night when round about midnight three friends from Kalawthaw village and a cousin of mine came and woke me up. They told me that several bullock carts carrying paddy from the fields to Kamawet village were on the road and wanted to know if I would join them in holding up the carts and making off with the paddy. I told them I had no stomach for such an undertaking, but they would not take no for an answer. I kept protesting, but they insisted, saying that they needed my help. Finally the fact that my cousin was a party to the proposed robbery decided me and I threw in my lot with them.

There were a great many carts carrying the paddy to Kamawet village that night and for a long time we were unable to catch any stragglers. Nevertheless, at about 4 a.m. we saw two carts coming along the road by themselves and were able to stop them. There were three men on the carts. After tying them up we drove away the carts at top speed.

When we came to an open field we unyoked the oxen and released them. We had intended to let the cartmen also go free when we had taken them far enough, but they must have thought that we were about to kill them, for we had hardly gone 50 yards when one of them made a break for it. Since his escape would mean disaster to all of us, one of us immediately gave chase, but as the terrified man was fleeing for his life it was only after about 800 yards that he was caught. The man who had to chase him was so enraged that he cut down the cartman on the spot with his sword. He then returned to us and said "I have killed the one that ran away. Now we cannot afford to let these others live, they have witnessed what happened to their companion." So saying, he fell upon the remaining two prisoners and slew them. By that time it was morning.

At about three o'clock on the following afternoon the police from Mudon arrived at our village. The Missing Persons report had been filed with them by the people of Kamawet. They summoned the Headman and organized a search for the cartmen and at four in the evening a body was uncovered. As the scene of the crime was so close to my hut the police immediately arrested me and started grilling me. I denied all knowledge of the crime and loudly declared my innocence. The next morning they made me accompany them in their search for the bodies of the two remaining cartmen. My cousin was not included in the search party. Our three accomplices were from another village, so suspicion did not fall on them. The police had no grounds for holding me, other than the proximity of my hut to where they had recovered the corpse and they had to release me the next day. A month passed by without any further developments.

Then one day the police received news that gambling was going on in Kalawthaw village and carried out a raid, in which one of the original five robbers, Kyaw Sein was arrested. At Mudon Police Station the police instead of confining their interrogation to gambling, began to question the men they had arrested for possible complicity in the murders. They pretended to have certain and unimpeachable information implicating them and Kyaw Sein fell into the trap. He made a complete confession, naming the rest of us as his accomplices. My cousin and I were arrested at 9 o'clock in the evening and the others round about midnight.

We were taken to Mudon that very night and placed in the same cell as Kyaw Sein. We did not know that by then Kyaw Sein had turned informer. In the cell Kyaw Sein told us that as one month had elapsed since the crime had taken place, he could easily get us off and that we should let him act as our spokesman. He said that the police were willing to co-operate with us. As Kyaw Sein could speak Burmese very fluently while the rest of us could hardly understand one word out of three we left all the talking to him during the police interrogation. Whenever he turned to us for confirmation of what he was saying we would nod our heads and say "that's right, that's right". When we were taken before a magistrate in Mudon too we continued to repeat "that's right".

When we arrived at the district capital Moulmein, we were separated from Kyaw Sein. He was kept in the Central Lock-up while we were sent to the main prison. My father came along to Moulmein and hired a lawyer for me. However, this lawyer could speak only Burmese while we spoke only Mon. When the magistrate examined us there was a mon interpreter present but we were told that since we had made a complete confession before the Mudon magistrate, we would not be permitted to change our story.

Accordingly, the Moulmein Sessions Judge sentenced us to 25 years each on two charges of dacoity and manslaughter (Section 369).

I was arrested in the month of January, 1948, just a few days after the country gained independence. Since being sentenced on the 7th of August in the same year I have served seven years in prison. My cousin was just 14 years old when the crime was committed and so was sent to the Borstal Training School instead. Two of the others are in Insein Jail, while one is in Rangoon Central Prison.

When I first came here I served as an apprentice in the sewing and tailoring department. After that I transferred to the carpentry shop. I have learned the carpenter's trade properly and if I am fortunate enough to be released I will take up carpentry for a living. I have never quarrelled with anyone in the prison and have always behaved well. I have repented of my crime long ago, but since my sentence is so long I don't know when I shall be released.

*

Because of his good record in prison, his steady pursuit of education and his hard work in the carpentry shop, Lay was granted a remission of his sentence for good behaviour and was released from prison in September, 1957. I encountered Lay on one of my trips to Rangoon and was overjoyed to see him outside. During my stay in prison Lay had served me faithfully and well, and had consequently been one of my closest and most trusted associates.

Lay's young wife had been faithful to him for seven whole years, struggling along as well as she could to support herself and their little child while he was in jail. When he walked out of prison she was waiting for him outside the prison gates with the child in her arms.

V
THE VAGRANT

Noticing a young man of about 18 years working assiduously at his prison chores, I made enquiries and found out that his name was Maung Tin Aung. In response to my appeal he related the following story of his life.

*

I was born in Mahlaing Htantaw Village, Meiktila District. My father died when I was very young and I have no recollection of him, whatsoever. In fact I do not think that I have even set eyes on him. I cannot even remember his name. They tell me that my mother was called Ma Aye Yi.

*

I lived on Pwezadan Quarter in Mahlaing with U Aung Lun, who was supposed to be my uncle, Ma Aye Yi's brother. I considered Ma Aye Yi to be my natural mother, but some people say that I was adopted by her. This is quite possible. Sometime ago, when they divided her estate, they claimed that I was an adopted son and therefore not entitled to any part of the inheritance. Accordingly, I did not receive a single pya when she died.

I am told that Ma Aye Yi was first married to a bottle washer named Ah Chun who worked in a Chinese bar and that I was born of their union.

When I was a boy I had to live in Thahpangan village with U Aung Lun's younger sister Ma Aye Kyi. When I reached the age of nine, U Aung Lun took me to live with him in Mahlaing Htandaw village. I attended the monastic school in the village for about three years, during which time I learned to read and write. During the Japanese occupation of Burma a Japanese cavalry unit was billeted in our village and I was given the job of sweeping the stables.

When the British reoccupied the country we bartered fresh eggs for sardines, cheese and other tinned foods with the British troops. One day I happened to beg a shirt from a Scottish sergeant in the Royal Air Force to replace the tattered one that I had on. The sergeant's name was Jack and he turned out to be a very kindly soul. He took me straight to his unit where he gave me a singlet and a pair of trousers. I stayed with him for a few weeks during which time I was not called upon to do any work whatsoever. I ate very well, Jock feeding me such delicacies as corn flakes and sausages.

Before long, Jack's unit was transferred, first to Meiktila and one month later to Maymyo, where I accompanied him. At Maymyo I met Jock's superior officer Mr. Blake who enrolled me in the Colgate High School on Mission Road. He also left five hundred kyats for me with the Headmistress Daw Chit Bu when his unit was repatriated.

The Headmistress at first took me into her home. Every Sunday I had to attend church, after which I went to the movies. I failed to do my homework regularly and received so many bad report cards that Daw Chit Bu finally decided that it would be better for me if I were admitted as a boarding student at the school. At the hostel we were required to attend Sunday school, where the pastor U Ko Ko Gyi taught us about Jacob, Esau, Mary, angels and other such matters. When I passed the fourth standard, Daw Chit Bu made me accompany her to the National Baptist Convention that was held that summer in Meiktila. The convention lasted for two days, at the end of which I was given leave to visit my uncle U Aung Lun in Mahlaing. When I arrived at U Aung Lun's house I learnt that my mother had died.

While in Maymyo the Headmistress had taken me aside one day and given me an accounting of the money that had been left for me by Jack and Mr. Blake. The five hundred kyats had been already spent on my board and lodging and my education and I discovered that she had been supporting me from her own pocket for some time. She admonished me, urging me to apply more diligence to my studies. However, I did not realise the true value of education at that time, thinking only of the imagined hardships of boarding school life and after I reached my uncle's village decided not to return to Maymyo.

In Mahlaing I worked as an apprentice in the Hla Ngwe motor

workshop for two months, at the end of which period I managed to get a ride on a truck bound for Rangoon.

In the whole of Rangoon town there were only two people I knew, namely Han Sein and Tin Sein from Maymyo. Unfortunately I did not know their address and even though the truck driver and other people tried their best to help me, my efforts to locate them proved unavailing.

At first I struck up an acquaintance with two women who earned their living by vending mangofruit, plums, betel-quids and cigarettes in front of the Sher Cinema Hall. They were quite poor and had a year old baby to support, but they gave me two meals. They also provided me with a place where I could sleep that night undisturbed by police patrols.

The next day I left them, feeling reluctant to impose on their hospitality much further and struck up an acquaintance with some boys near the Burmese Agency offices. With them I entered upon a new and carefree existence. We would spend each afternoon and evening in idling around near the cinema halls, looking at the various posters. When the lights were turned off after the last show we crept into the dark corners to sleep. We had no blankets and slept in the clothes which we had on.

At eight o'clock in the morning, when the cinema halls were opened for cleaning and airing we would help the sweepers to sweep the theatre. For this service we were permitted to sift the sweepings for cigarette studs and other odds and ends that may have been left in the hall. After this we would proceed to the Burma Athletic Association Football ground to pick up some more cigarette stubs. When we had accumulated enough of these, we took them to the Chinese opium dens on 23rd Street and sold them to the Chinese who extracted the tobacco for re-rolling into new cigarettes. We were paid up to eight annas for every tin of stubs. Sometimes we would rummage among the dust bins near the football grounds for any discarded items that might concievably have a resale value.

We would eat at a shop that sold left-over foods from nearby hotels. Here we could get a really satisfying meal for only eight annas. If we did not have this amount, we could still choose the cheaper dishes which would cost as little as one anna for the entire meal. This shop was patronised by opium addicts, wayside vendors and masseurs.

Every morning, around eight o'clock, I would slip away to the Royal Lakes and bathe there and wash my clothes with the pieces of soap that had been left behind by previous bathers. I would spread out my clothes on the grass until they were dry after which I would dress and come back to town.

For entertainment I would go and see cheap reruns of old movies, government sponsored free shows which featured news-reels and open air Anyein dances. This life in Rangoon was not an easy one, but it had the advantage over village life in that I could see many more dances and film shows.

When the Hpa-Hsa-Pa-La Quarter burned down, I went to the gutted area to look for corrugated iron sheets, copper and lead pieces. I sold the lead for K 3-50 per viss, while copper fetched only K 2-50 pyas.

One day I met a worker named Yacoob from a tea-shop in Moghul Street and through him got a job with a jeweller named Daw Mya Thein. At this time I had been living on the streets for nearly 8 months.

Daw Mya Thein lived in a house on Pagoda Road where I was employed as a servant, my duties consisting mainly of shopping for groceries and helping in the kitchen. My salary was twenty kyats a month. Every Sunday I was given the day off and I used to either go fishing or see a movie show. After about seven months I grew dissatisfied with Daw Mya Thein's treatment of me and I left her employment.

I had thirty-five kyats in cash and four or five sets of clothing when I left her house. I took the train to Mahlaing and went to stay with my uncle. Three months later I returned to Rangoon.

In Rangoon I met three friends who urged me either to join the Army or the Rehabilitation Brigade with them. We decided on the latter and were accepted by the recruitment officers.

Upon enlistment we were first given basic military training, after which we were asked to state our preference as to the trade we would like to follow. I chose carpentry. We were paid a monthly wage of K 82/-, of which K 37/- was deducted for uniform and messing. Our commanding officer was a man called Mondaing (cyclone) Ye Din. The company commander was Lieutenant Hla Win.

Two months later I left the Brigade and returned to Rangoon and presented myself at the Army Induction Centre at Myenigon. However, I did not pass the medical examination and was turned down by the Board.

I moved back into the city and resumed my previous life, scavenging for cigarette butts and other odds and ends. As I gained more experience I began to learn which objects fetched the best prices and which were a drug on the market. I also found out the preferences of different dealers. I soon began to earn more and in keeping with my increased income, I changed my eating place. The shop I chose was situated at the corner of Lathar Street and 21st Street. Here one could get a square meal for 30 pyas. After dinner I would go to a corner of the Rangoon General Hospital where I could get a glass of sherbet for five pyas.

One day I met three acquaintances near the Co-operative's warehouse. I had been intending to see a movie, but when they told me that they had been hired by U Polo, the proprietor of a theatrical troupe, to move his stage effects from the premises of the Thayettaw Monastery I decided to accompany them. For our services U Polo gave us a good meal and two kyats each. The others considered that they had been underpaid and went away dissatisfied. U Polo and his wife liked the way I worked and offered me a job with their troupe which I willingly accepted. My duties were light, but I did not like the way the proprietor's wife treated me. She would make me run errands for her and at times scold me severely. Finally, I could stand it no longer and left their employ just before the scheduled performance at the Mogaung Pagoda Festival.

One afternoon I met a friend named Shwe Win alias Shwe Kyay and his brother Mya Win. They were both working in a restaurant. After having a meal with them I got up and helped to clear the table and wash the dishes. The proprietor of the restaurant, U Ba Thin and his wife Daw Ma Ma Gyi observed this and offered me a job in the shop. The next day I went to work for them for twenty kyats a month and free meals.

Shwe Kyay had come to Rangoon, with the intention of joining the Army and was unhappy working in this place. At his urging I took him one day into the heart of the city and showed him the zoo, the Central Jail, the Army Recruitment Centre and other places of interest. On our return to the restaurant in the evening we were scolded by Daw Ma Ma Gyi for absenting ourselves without permission. Shwe Kyay was quite upset and left the shop to go to Kongyan by train. However, he neglected to buy a ticket and was arrested for ticketless travel and sentenced to fifteen days imprisonment. When he was released from jail he reappeared at the restaurant, where his brother Mya Win gave him some money to proceed to Pyu, where they had some relatives. From these relatives Shwe Kyay managed to borrow enough money to enable him to return to Mahlaing.

In spite of their promise to pay me a salary of twenty kyats a month, the proprietor of the restaurant paid me only ten kyats. The shop was built on the sidewalk, in contravention of municipal laws and had been ordered dismantled. For these reasons and also because I could get a better paid job in an Indian shop, I decided to leave them. Before long, I quit the job, without bothering to ask them again for the ten kyats they owed me.

Making my way to an ice-cream and sherbert shop located at the corner of Fraser and Montgomery Streets, I asked the owner if he could find some work for me. He told me that there was no opening in Rangoon, but that he could place me in a job if I were willing to go to Prome. I assured him that I was and so he sent me there to work in the Pakistan Hotel on Lanmadaw Road. The monthly salary was K 30/- which was increased to K 35/- the next month. The work was quite demanding. I had to get up early in the morning to sweep the floor and wash the tables. I had to manipulate the ice-cream churn, wash the pots and pans and kill a basketfull of chickens every day. It was rarely that I got to sleep before midnight.

At the end of four months I asked for a raise but was turned down and so I left this job as well. I had seventy kyats in savings. Having become somewhat disenchanted with Rangoon I decided not to return there and went back to Mahlaing instead.

When I arrived at Mahlaing, U Aung Lun cautioned me against associating with Shwe Kyay. I did not heed his advice and when he scolded me I left his house and went to live with Shwe Kyay. My friend's father U Sein Khaing hired out his bullock cart for a living and Shwe Kyay would often have to drive the cart. However, whenever Shwe Kyay recieved five kyats for the bullock cart hire he would spend four kyats on cigarettes handing over only one kyat to his parents. I helped U Sein Khaing to drive the bullocks, to feed them and tend to them. After a while, I ran out of money for movies and other minor expenditures and decided that I could no longer stay there. Accordingly I stopped a truck on the highway and managed to get a lift back to Rangoon.

In the city I went looking for work and finally got a job in a roadside Chinese chow mein shop. My duties in that shop were to wait on the tables and to wash the dishes. Since the shop stayed open all night I found the work very tiring. After about fifteen days I quarreled with another worker in the shop and left.

Being out of a job I had to make the most of what little money I had left. One afternoon, at about three p.m., I was sitting on a bench in Bandoola Park. Two other men were seated near me. Suddenly, two men on bicycles approached. They stopped and asked us where we were from. The other two replied that they were dockyard labourers and produced papers to prove it. When they came to me, I confessed that I was unemployed. "In that case come with me, I will get you a job", said one and thinking that he really meant it, I hopped onto the carrier of his bicycle and went along with him. Only when we arrived at the Kyauktada Police Station and I was thrown into the lock-up did I find out that the two were policemen and that the man who had arrested me was Sergeant Ko Than Lwin of the vagrancy detail.

The next day I was arraigned before the East Rangoon Special Magistrate U Percy Mya Maung. After three months of repeated delays my case was finally heard and I was sentenced to six months imprisonment. My sentence will run out on 3-2-56.

I do not know what I shall do when I am released. I will take any job I can get. If I cannot get work I will return to my village. I have resolved never to be caught again without a job. I shall never forget the hardships of these last seven months in jail.

VI
BOYS' HOME

It was a sad spectacle to see Maung Kyaw Win in prison. He was a young lad just turned sixteen when I first met him in Rangoon Central Jail.

His story :

I do not remember the date of my birth. My father is Shan and my mother Burmese. Father's name is Ko Hla Pe and mother's name is Ma Thaung Kyi. They both come from Kanyon village in Tavoy District. Before the War father worked in the tin mines belonging to Naung Lu Pe. Mother was an itinerant vegetable seller.

Finding it difficult in Tavoy to make both ends meet, my parents decided to move to Pahton village in Moulmein district. It was in this village that my brother, my sister and I were born. After struggling to make a living in Moulmein for a few years, my parents returned to Tavoy to seek employment on the Tavoy foreshore. We were left behind in Pahton village with relatives.

When the Second World War broke out my elder brother, then 17 years old, immediately enlisted in the Burma Independence Army. My parents sent word that my sister and I were to join them in Tavoy. My sister obeyed, but I remained in Pahton village, being only 3 years old at that time and my aunt having become very attached to me did not wish to let me go.

A year after the Japanese had occupied the country my parents wrote to us informing us that my brother was in Rangoon and that he was already married. After the British reoccupation we received another letter from them, stating that they had given away my sister in marriage.

I was unhappy having to live apart from my parents, and so accompanied some professional gamblers to the Mergui Pagoda festival where I helped them operate their gambling booths. A month later the motor sampan on which we travelled put in at Tavoy, where I deserted the gamblers. While swimming one day with three or four companions, some workers on a motor sampan asked us if we would like to come along with them on a trip to Rangoon as deck-hands, and I jumped at the idea. After an uneventful trip we wound up in Rangoon.

When we docked I was given fifty kyats in wages and decided to spend it on some new clothes. However, once ashore I met with an automobile accident and almost lost my life. On top of this the driver of the motor vehicle got down and beat me up. Feeling quite despondent I decided not to go back to Tavoy on the motor sampan.

After drifting about in Rangoon for a while I finally returned overland to Moulmein where I found my relatives in a fever of anxiety over my fate, some having already concluded that I had come to an untimely end.

My aunts took me by motor sampan to Tavoy where I received bad news. My father had eloped with a young woman and had left for Kayan leaving my mother and my young brother to fend for themselves. This they had been unable to do, with the result that after a while the elders had taken pity on her and married her off to a Chinese merchant named U Hpyan. Ten months after this she had had to undergo an operation at the Central Women's Hospital near the Gymkhana Club in Rangoon. She was at present still in hospital.

I was greatly depressed at these developments and did not know what to do next. My aunts put their heads together and decided that it would be best to take me back to Rangoon.

U Hpyan lived in a house on 11th street, and as soon as we arrived in Rangoon we went to see him. He took us on a visit to the hospital to see my mother, and then put us up in his home. A month later my aunts returned to Moulmein leaving me with my stepfather. Mother had still not yet been discharged from hospital when they left.

U Hpyan wanted to educate me and accordingly took me to the Thayet-taw Monastery and entrusted me to the care of the Abbot of Than-yar-wa-si monastic school. However I was completely uninterested in school work. When I was unable to recite my lessons the Abbot would say nothing, but the monk assisting him would freely resort to the cane and before long I began staying away from school. Three months after I was first enrolled the Abbot passed away, and fearing that without his restraining influence I was due for even severer punishment at the hands of his assistant, refused to attend school any longer. U Hpyan was very annoyed at this and one day lost his temper and gave me a stiff beating. My mother was still in hospital and feeling that in her continued absence I was bound to be beaten more often in future, I ran away from home.

Before long I had landed a job as a paid apprentice at the Kyaw Than Motor Workshop on Morton Street. Within six months I had picked up a fair working knowledge of automobile maintenance.

Although the proprietor of the workshop was U Kyaw Than, the man who was really running the day to day operation of the workshop was his manager Ko Tin Aye. There were three or four other apprentices senior to me who were about nineteen years of age. I was still thirteen. We did not have much dealings with U Kyaw Than, our training being left in the hands of Ko Tin Aye. Ko Tin Aye was like a bigbrother to all of us.

One evening, after U Kyaw Than went home, Ko Tin Aye asked us to dismantle a car that had been left for repair by a rich Chinese merchant. We removed the tyres and the engine, and Ko Tin Aye had the chassis repainted. The registration number on the engine was also altered, He then had everything taken away. We learned later that he had sold the car to a buyer from Sanchaung.

After we had helped him with the job, Ko Tin Aye took us to a restaurant and gave us a fine meal, after which he treated us to a movie show. When the movie was over, he invited us to spend the night in his house. We were quite happy to do so.

Shortly after midnight the police raided the place. Ko Tin Aye had decamped, and his wife kept insisting that she did not know his whereabouts. The three of us were placed under arrest and had to spend the remainder of the night in the Bar Street Lock-up.

In the morning I was asked how old I was, and not wishing to be separated from my companions, I replied that I was nineteen years old. However the police surgeon who examined me declared that I was only thirteen years old and I was accordingly sent to the Home for Waifs and Strays near Inya Lake pending the outcome of the trial.

Ko Tin Aye had escaped, and a warrant was out for his arrest. At the trial the two other apprentices who had helped him were given prison sentences of three months each. I was given twenty lashes of the cane, but in view of my youth the cane used was a school cane and I did not find it too painful. The boys in the home had coached me properly and at the trial I had thrown myself on the mercy of the court, submitting that I had only carried out orders and was too young to have understood what was going on. The judge must have believed me to have meted out such lenient punishment, and I am very grateful to my friends at the home of their advice.

U Kyaw Than appeared on all our trial days. He assured us that he would do all in his power to have our sentences reduced. When I was released I made my way back to his workshop, since I had nowhere else to go, and he engaged me once again as an apprentice.

At the end of three months, the warrant issued for the arrest of Ko Tin Aye expired, and he was still at large. However one day U Kyaw Than met him face to face on the Insein-Rangoon bus on which he had been working. U Kyaw Than immediately whipped out a dagger and attacked Tin Aye, the knife striking him a glancing blow on the chest. Ko Tin Aye was hospitalised while Ko Kyaw Than was arrested and then released on bail. I worked on at Kyaw Than Motor Workshop for another three months and then left.

My mother had been discharged from hospital and she and my stepfather had moved to a house in Kamayut. I joined them there. At that time my young brother had reached the age of ten. My mother had not had any children by my stepfather.

While living in Kamayut she obtained a job at the Zamani Umbrella Works. Her husband sold sweetmeats at a Chinese Shop in Chinatown. He also found me a job at a Chinese restaurant. Although the pay was good, being forty five kyats a month with meals thrown in, I was not happy there and after a month gave up the job to go and live with a friend on Goodliffe Road.

This person was a bus driver with whom I had become acquainted when he had brought his bus to the Kyaw Than workshop for repairs. He was eighteen years old and already married. His wife sold betel and cigarettes in front of the Thwin Cinema. I helped them by hawking the cigarettes inside the cinema hall. They did not pay me and I did not demand payment either. They fed me and bought me some clothes. I lived with them for three months, until my mother learned of my whereabouts and came to fetch me home.

Fearing that I would pick up bad habits if I stayed in Rangoon much longer, she sent me back to my aunt in Kanyon village, Tavoy District. My aunt enrolled me in the village school, but I could not work up any enthusiasm over it. I would play truant as often as possible, and finally after five months had passed, I stole one hundred and fifty kyats from her and left for Rangoon by motor sampan.

In Rangoon I made the acquaintance of a twenty-one year old trishawman named Ko Ohn Maung. He took me home to meet his wife and child, and I spent one night at his house. Soon I became enamoured of the trishawman's life and begged him to get me a permit to operate a trishaw.

Ko Ohn Maung knew the inside ropes, and took me for the medical examination, where I gave my age as eighteen. When the time came for me to demonstrate my proficiency on a trishaw, Ko Ohn Maung took the test for me and I was passed with flying colours. He also coached me in the traffic rules and road etiquette and I had no difficulty in passing the required examination. In addition to the fee of twenty five kyats for the operator's licence I spent a considerable amount on tea for the clerks and petty officials in the Registration Department.

Ko Ohn Maung explained to me a few things about his profession. To be successful a trishawman had to be quick-witted and alert. He had to have a smattering of English and Hindi, and perhaps a little Chinese as well. He had to know the city thoroughly and be able to take his passengers straight-away to any address they mentioned. He also had to know the location of the principal brothels in the area. Ko Ohn Maung himself was a very successful trishawman. He knew all the brothels in the Lewis Street neighbourhood and had standing arrangements with them whereby he would steer customers to them for a consideration. In addition to the commission he earned from the brothels, he was usually given an extra tip by his passengers. Sailors were his best fares usually giving him five kyats for a trip. European sailors were even more generous, throwing in free meals and drinks as well. Ko Ohn Maung's daily earnings were sometimes as high as thirty kyats. On rainy days he would work only for as long as it took him to earn two kyats, the fee which he had to pay to the owner of the trishaw, after which he would take the day off fearing that he would catch a cold if he worked in bad weather.

I did not follow his example in plying my trishaw for the

brothel trade. I did not approve of this kind of work and anyway I was too young to be much good at it. Accordingly I moved to another trishaw stand where I was accepted after paying ten kyats for admission to the new trishawmen's association.

Working as an honest trishawman, I could earn a maximum of ten to twelve kyats a day. On some days I would not get a single fare and had to make up the owner's fee out of my own pocket. Whenever I obtained some money I would go and have a meal. Trishawmen lead a very strenous life and can eat like horses. Most of their earnings are spent on food.

During the summer and winter months I slept on the trishaw. When the rainy season came I rented a hut for twenty-five kyats a month. I had no companion with whom to share the hut and when I left for work in the morning I would leave it in the care of the Landlord, who fortunately lived in the same compound.

One summer night I went to see a movie. After the movie I decided it was too late to return home and went to sleep on a bench in Bandoola Park. During the night a police patrol appeared and rounded up all the people who were sleeping there. There were twelve boys of my age in the group and in the morning all twelve of us were sent to the Boys' Home in Golden Valley.

As soon as the police officer had left the home we were set upon by the previous inmates, stripped and beaten until we begged for mercy. The masters did not make a move to interfere, but stood at the second story window and looked with folded arms upon the scene below.

At this school we were not taught anything at all. Our days were taken up with chopping firewood, drawing water, and kitchen duties. We were not given enough to eat, and went perpetually hungry.

On the east of the school enclosure was a small pond where we had to launder our clothes, wash the dirty dishes, scour the pots and pans and take our baths. We also had to draw our drinking water from the same pond.

Conditions at this home were intolerable and far worse than in an ordinary prison. Whenever we took off our clothes we would see them crawling with scores of lice and other vermin, all bloated with our blood. On Christmas Day all of us were issued new clothes to wear.

However as soon as the last visitor had left the clothes were repossessed by the school authorities and we were made to put on our old clothes again. Every now and then some sympathetic donor would send us food and cakes and sweets, but we were not given even a whiff of these, being appropriated by the schoolmasters and their toadies.

The worst thing about the place however was the perennial fear in which we all went. There was back-biting and bullying of the worst sort, aided and abetted or least countenanced by the school authorities.

From the very day of my arrival I determined to escape from this reformatory. There were a few who had managed to get away from the grounds, but well-meaning individuals from outside had apprehended them and brought them back, thinking they were doing what was in the best interests of the boys and not realising, the hell to which they were returning the boys.

Six months later I made my attempt to escape, in the company of two other boys. The other two boys were caught and taken back to the institution. I was the only successful one and this was due to my going straight to the Boy's Home near Inya Lake where I had previously stayed and throwing myself on the mercy of "mother", the lady who ran the Home. This kind hearted lady listened with sympathy and obvious distress to my story and wept for me at its conclusion. She also readmitted me at once to her home.

This school was a great contrast to the one in Golden Valley. The children were all very happy under mother's care. They were polite and helpful and very considerate of each other. We were given clean clothes to wear and plenty of good food to eat. In addition to ordinary school subjects, we were taught carpentry and weaving and sports such as gymnastics. A boy who learnt carpentry was given five kyats a month for pocket money, while one who had learned weaving received ten kyats. Every Sunday we were given leave to go to the movies.

After seven happy months under "mother's" wing I went to her and told her that I wished to leave. She wrote out a discharge slip for me and armed with this I approached the A-1.Film Company for a job. The film studio gave me an audition where I had to demonstrate prowess in gymnastics. The director of the studio, U Chit Pe then offered me a job as a gardener, promising to give me a screen role when a suitable opportunity arose. He appeared to be sincere in his promise to me, since the current "stunt" actors Kyaw Nyunt and diving Tin Hla were also graduates of "Mother's Home", and I accordingly accepted the gardener's job.

While working as a gardener at the studios, I was called upon to play the role of a young boy who was working hand in glove with a magician, played by the actor Thaung Shwe. While Thaung Shwe had the attention of a crowd riveted on him, I had to snip off a gold necklace from a young woman. When she raised the alarm and the crowd gave chase, I had to run away, displaying my gymnastic prowess while doing so. Finally I had to climb a tall tree growing beside the Inya Lakes. When the police surrounded the tree and had me cornered, I made my escape by diving into the lakes from a great height and confounding my pursuers by not resurfacing at all. The final shot showed me handing over the gold necklace to the magician in a deserted house. My role depicted the youth of famous actor Shwe Ba, who carried on from where I left off in the movie.

This was the only role of my movie career. After reverting to my job as gardener for three months, I grew impatient at having to wait for another opportunity and resigned. I then went to the Rangoon Film Studios and applied for a job, only to be hired again as a gardener.

One month later I left this job also and was hired as an assitant by a goldsmith named Ko Thein Han who ran a shop near Pazundaung Market. One day Ko Thein Han asked me to take a tical of gold to an Indian goldsmith on 29th Street to have some work done on it. I located the Indian's shop with great difficulty, and by the time the work was finished some little time had elapsed. Meanwhile Ko Thein Han became convinced that I had absconded with the gold and reported the matter to the Police Station. When I returned with the gold and handed it to him I was immediately arrested.

The magistrate sentenced me to forty-five days rigorous imprisonment. He explained that he was being very lenient with me, since the maximum possible sentence for this crime was three years.

My brother has enlisted in the No. 16. Burma Regiment. When my sentence runs out, I plan to return to Kyaw Than Motor Workshop and ask for a job.

VII
THE QUIET ONE

Nineteen year old Maung Pu is short and dark skinned. He is a quiet well-mannered young boy who gets along well with the other prisoners.

Since I was on duty at Block No. 5 I took the opportunity one day to seek him out and ask him to relate to me the circumstances that led to his being in prison.

*

Maung Pu's narrative..........

I was born in Kamayut Township, Insein District. My father is U Ya Zin and my mother Dwa Sein Mya. Before the war my father worked as a clerk for the Burma Oil Company Refinery in Syriam at a salary of ninety kyats. When the war ended he entered the timber business as a commission agent. He is sixty two years old now. At present he is living at Thukayeiktha garden, Kamayut.

I have eight brothers and sisters. I am the second youngest in the family. My eldest brother Cassim is a bus-driver, another is an apprentice at the Insein Locomotive Shed, and a third works in the Thamaing Textile Factory as an unskilled labourer.

My brothers are still living with my parents and contributing to the family budget. Only the eldest has taken a wife. All my sisters have married and moved away.

When I was four years old I became a Moslem. My parents enrolled me in Dwa Tha Htet's school in Kamayut when I was eight. However, I studied in that school only up till the second grade, after which I withdrew from school and stayed at home for about two years.

By 1947-48 I had reached the age of thirteen and started working as a conductor, on my brother Cassim's bus. In 1948 I took out a bus conductor's license. When I started to work I was paid one kyat and fifty pyas a day and meals. Our bus was the "Khin San Yin" and had the Rangoon-Insein run. Within a year I was earning three kyats a day. Sometime after that the bus-owner increased my daily wages to five kyats, since I had become quite proficient in getting passengers and had also picked up some knowledge of car engine repair and maintenance. I worked as a conductor for three years, after which I took out a driver's license and was engaged by a rich chinese who lived next door to us, to drive his jeep-taxi. Besides being provided with meals, I was given a monthly salary of ninety kyats. At the end of six months my salary was increased to one hundred kyats. I worked for him for one year and eight months, after which I left the job.

I was then sent to Toungoo with three others by an umbrella manufacturer named U Pyone Cho of Hlaing Road to learn the craft of making umbrella rods. During our apprenticeship we had to put in twelve hours of work a day for four months. When we returned to Rangoon we were hired at six kyats a day by U Pyone Cho, who made us work in a separate section of his factory, so that no one else could learn the craft by watching us.

The umbrella rods were not made of wood, but from the vine of the Sagawar that was obtained from the Ngathaing-gyaung area. These were sent to us in length of nine to ten feet which we cut to the required sizes when they arrived at Kamayut. The rods that we made were delivered in bulk to E.C. Madha's umbrella factory, and to other Indian concerns on 30th, 35th and 40th streets at the rate of K8-50 pyas per dozen for the men's umbrella size and K5-00 pyas per dozen for the ladies' umbrella size.

After a while the manufacture of these rods became very popular in the Kamayut area. They were in great demand by the umbrella factory and practically everyone tried his hand at making them. Of the four of us who had gone to Toungoo for apprenticeship, Maung Win left when his uncle offered to set him up in a shop of his own and Maung Tin was also persuaded by his relatives to leave us. Only Aye Maung and I were left with U Pyone Cho. By this time the art of making umbrella rods was no longer a secret in Kamayut.

One day there was a funeral in the house of some neighbours. These people were so poor that they could not even offer cheroots and betel to visitors who came to console with them. The deceased was Daw Mya Tin, and she left behind three daughters. There were so few visitors to their home that it did not even resemble a funeral house, so I went and hired a light for K 3/- and taking it to their home, installed it for them. I also bought a pack of cards and waited for some people to come and keep the daughters company by playing cards throughout the night, while waiting for others to appear. I whiled away the time by playing cards with the three girls for match-sticks.

At about 8 p.m. a man named Ko Soe Tin entered. He was drunk. In his hand he held a wad of notes. Lurching his way to the table he said "I place a bet of K 300/-" I explained to him that we were playing for matchsticks and asked him to wait for the others if he wanted to gamble. He shouted that he wanted to play, and insisted that I accept his bet. When I replied that I could not do so, he raised his foot and kicked me between the shoulders. I demanded to know why he had assaulted me and he replied : "I kicked you because I wanted to know what do you want to do about it" and followed it up by kneeing me. Unable to control myself any longer, I ran to my house, which was only about 50 yards away, grabbed an axe and running back to where he was, chopped at him. he turned and tried to fend off the blow but the blade sliced through his forearm, leaving it attached to the upper arm only by a piece of skin. My next blow hit one eye and the right side of his face. He fell in a heap.

The whole village knew of our quarrel, but no one reported the matter to the police, because Soe Tin had made himself extremely unpopular in the neighbourhood by bullying others, and making a nuisance of himself especially when drunk.

He was taken to Insein Hospital for treatment of his injuries. After five days he recovered consciousness and immediately named me as his assailant. The Insein police came and asked me to come to Insein police station for questioning. Before going along with the police I contacted the A.F.P.F.L. president U Ba Kyi. U Ba Kyi and three or four others accompanied me to the police station, where I made a complete confession. I was charged under section 324 and granted bail immediately.

Two months after the quarrel Soe Tin was discharged from hospital, and the case was heard before the 4th Addition Magistrate. The hearings went on for a month. There was not a single witness willing to testify on his behalf. All the witnesses supported me.

However, since I had not denied my part in the affair I was found guilty as charged. But as Soe Tin admitted being drunk at the time and it was apparent that he had been at fault, the judge sentenced me to only two years imprisonment. Since Insein Jail was meant only for habitual criminals and those serving long sentences, I was sent to Rangoon Jail.

While in prison I received a letter from Soe Tin in which he admitted his fault. He stated that he had moved to Sanchaung from Kamayut. I learnt later that he had been forced to leave the neighbourhood due to the hostility of the residents who all blamed him for my imprisonment. My appeal to the Sessions Court resulted in my sentence being reduced to eighteen months.

I have gone into debt to fight my case, and when I am released from prison I will have to go back to making umbrella rods to pay off my creditors.

VIII
THE GAMBLER

At the time of my detention in Rangoon Central Jail the minors in the prison were segregated from the adult prisoners and housed in their own quarters near the Hospital Building. However a few of them had to come everyday to the central kitchens to fetch food for the rest.

Maung Soe Tin was an adolescent boy who did not appear to be more than seventeen. He and two or three companions would stop by every morning on their way to the kitchens to watch us playing golf on the prison mini-course. At first they kept chattering away while we were addressing the ball, until we explained to them the need for utter silence so as not to disturb the concentration of the players.

Maung Soe Tin seemed to show more interest in the game than the others. Without our bidding he would come and shoulder our golf bags, smooth out the browns, hunt for lost balls, and generally make himself useful on the course.

This lad soon aroused my curiosity. He seemed to be quick and alert, and even though he appeared to be of no more than high school age, his demeanour and his conversation indicated a wide and varied experience belied by his youthful looks. This prompted me to question him regarding his past, and the following is the result of my inquiries.

*

My real name is Maung Soe Tin. This is not the name by which I am known by the police or the prison authorities, to whom I gave my name as Maung Tin.

I have never lived with my father and I did not even know his name, let alone set eyes on him, until just a few years ago. His name is Ko Mya Than. My mother's name is Ma Ohn Kyi.

My mother gave birth to seven children, but with 3 different husbands. My elder sister had one father, I had another, and the remaining five children had a third.

After my mother separated from her first husband she married my father. Three months before I was born she divorced him and married again. Until this day I have not learned the cause of their separation. My father is still alive and has another wife.

When I was 8 or 9 years old I asked mother where my father lived. She told me his name and gave me an address near the Myenigon Football Grounds. I looked up the address and met my father and his sisters who lived there. I made frequent visits to their house thereafter.

I was 3 years old when my mother married again. My stepfather Ko Ba Sein was 5 years her junior, and I called him Ako or "Elder Brother" instead "Father". I did not approve of her marriage to him, and there was little love lost between us.

One day my stepfather beat me so severely that my uncle picked up a sword and chased him. He ran out out of the house and took shelter with his master in Ahlone. Shortly after this the Allied bombing of Rangoon became greatly intensified, and fearing that a British invasion would find us caught between opposing forces, we moved out of the city and took refuge in Aye Ywa, village opposite Kemmendine. My stepfather remained in Ahlone.

When the war ended we returned to Kemmedine where my uncle set up a very successful business as a barber. To please my mother, my uncle went to Ahlone and brought back my stepfather. As soon as he entered the house my elder sister left by the back door. She could not stand the sight of him. Before long she eloped with her sweetheart.

Two months later, mother persuaded her to return home. However as soon as she entered, my stepfather left the house by the back door. My sister and I bitterly upbraided my mother for not loving us and of thinking only of her husband's welfare, but to no avail. Before long they had moved out of my uncle's house and into a house on the police station road. My uncle insisted that I accompany them, and this I had to do inspite of my heated protests.

When I was 9 years old my mother entered a lottery and bought three winning tickets, receiving prizes of 3 gold sovereigns for one ticket, 2 gold sovereigns for the second, and one gold sovereign and 50 kyats for the third.

Within 3 days my mother had arranged to conduct a Shinpyu or Buddhist novitiation ceremony for me.

About a month later I found the sum of forty kyats under the mattress of a monk, and together with another novice, went and spent fifteen kyats of it on food and drink. When we got back to the monastery we were soundly beaten as a result of which I ran away from the monastery. I wandered around the neighbourhood aimlessly, begging for food and sleeping wherever I could find shelter until one day I met my mother on the road and she forced me to return with her to the monastery where I formally ended my novitiation and I was divested of my robe.

I was then enrolled in a secular school where I passed the second standard examination. Shortly after this I stayed away from school for two whole days. When my uncle heard of this he was enraged, and tying me hand and foot beat me with a cane until my whole body was a mass of welts and bruises. Five days later, when the wounds had somewhat healed, I ran away from the house.

I did not have a single pya in my pocket, but I did not care so long as I got away. I took shelter in a small wayside rest-house near the Pegu Bridge. At this rest-house I met five boys who were roughly my age, that is about ten years old. They gave their names as Mahamed, Mamoot, Maung Maung, Po Hto and Ohn Maung. These boys shared their food with me and took me to the movies with them. There was a man about 30 years old who lived in the rest-house with them. His name was Ko San Shwe and he was an opium addict. He held the boys completely under his sway and was living on the proceeds of the petty crimes that he forced them to commit on his behalf but of this at first I knew nothing.

Within four or five days I had learned from the boys how to pilfer and steal. I entered into the spirit of the thing, because, among other things, I knew that they would not feed me indefinitely without some contribution on my part. Also, they went in fear of Ko San Shwe, to whom they had to turn over everything they managed to steal, on pain of physical torture such as having a sharp chisel thrust into their sides or a hot iron placed against their limbs. All of the boys had scars which bore mute testimony to San Shwe's savagery.

I had no use for a man who took advantage of weakness of young boys, and gradually began to dissociate myself from the group. In this I was abetted by an Indo-Burmese boy named Mohamet. Before long we began to stay away from the rest-house at nights, choosing to sleep in the bazaar instead.

San Shwe did not like this, and took to muttering dark threats whenever he met us in town. One day, just before the commencement of the Shwemawdaw Pagoda Festival he went to the police and reported that the two of us were young pick-pockets who should not be left at large during the festivities. The police were rounding up all known petty criminals at the time, and Mohamet and I found ourselves placed behind bars for 14 days.

When we were brought before a magistrate I related to him all that I knew about San Shwe's mode of living and apparently convinced him of the truth of my story, for he released us after assuring us that if we could produce sufficient evidence against San Shwe, he would have him summarily arrested and thrown in jail.

Ten days later San Shwe and his gang were evicted from their rest-house and moved into our territory on the platform of the Shwemawdaw Pagoda. We first saw the five boys he had brought with him and drove them off with blows and curses. After the boys had fled we went in search of San Shwe, reasoning correctly that he could not be far away. I had an iron poker in my hand and Mohamet had a two-by-one piece of wood, and when we found him sleeping in one corner of a stairway we straightaway attacked him. We managed to land only three times on the head, most of our blows falling on his hands and body. After this we made our escape, Mohamet taking the train to Rangoon while I got a lift on a lorry going upcountry to Pyu.

I spent the night at the Pyu Railway station alone on the platform and in the morning was sitting feeling lost and hungry when a couple approached and asked me where I was from. I told them that I had run away from home and that I did not have any money with which to buy food. They felt very sorry for me and urged me to come and live with them offering to adopt me and take good care of me and I gratefully accepted.

Ko Sán Mya and Ma Nyein were indigent cultivators from Setkon village, 16 miles east of Pyu, who had come to town to buy general provisions. Both of them had had previous marriages, and they already had a total of six children by their former spouses but in the bigness of their hearts there was room for one more child.

I lived with them happily for two seasons, after which old ladies passing through the village appealed to my foster parents to let them have one child for adoption. Ko San Mya and Ma Nyein asked me how I felt about the matter, and when I indicated that I was willing to go along with the old ladies they reluctantly gave their consent.

After six or seven days in my new home, during which I had to help the two women in the bazaar, I decided that I did not want to live any further with them and took the next train to Rangoon without saying anything to them.

When I arrived in Rangoon I contacted neither my mother nor my uncle but instead went to the Moghul street mosque area and joined the street urchins who roamed the vicinity and slept on the pavements at night. I told them that I was from Pegu and that I had run away from home. They welcomed me into their ranks, dubbing me the "Peguan" that is "the one from Pegu".

One of these boys, whom the others called *Kala dawe* was very adept at breaking and entering, and he took my training in hand. About a month after we started working together we come upon a textile shop near the Moghul Street Bank, which had a small rear window open through which we could extract bolts of textiles. On the first day we got away with 8 bolts, on the second day with 10, and the next day with 14. Each of these was worth between fifty and seventy-five kyats.

On the fourth night, while I was on watch outside, Kaladawe was surprised by a police patrol. The police questioned him and then let him go, keeping the textile goods for themselves. They even kept my longyi with which we had bundled up the textiles, and I had to sleep in my underwear that night.

The following Sunday Kaladawe and I, together with two accomplices broke into a crockery shop on the same street and took K 310/- from the cash box. From inside that shop we managed to enter the adjoining shop where we found 36 table clocks which we divided among ourselves. I went all the way to Bahan to sell my share of nine clocks for 18 kyats each, after which I went to sleep at my grand-mother's house in Kemmendine. The other three remained in the Moghul street area.

At 10 O'clock in the morning the police arrested Kaladawe and found some of the stolen goods in his possession. He implicated us, and the other two were picked up in short order. When they came for me at Kemmendine I managed to give them the slip and the next morning I took the train to Pyinmana.

At Pyawbwe Station I met a group of five or six beggars, all adults, who took pity on me when they heard my story, and took me with them to their small village near the Pyawbwe Cemetery. There were about 20 beggars, both male and female living in their camp and they all welcome me with open arms. In a short while they had became very fond of me, and I on my part had became very attached to them.

About a month later they invited me to join them on their begging trips, but I declined. However I made up for this by helping around the camp, carrying water, chopping wood and doing odd jobs for them, and they were quite satisfied. I was happy with my friends and lived with them for over two years.

In time, however, I began to miss my relatives in Rangoon, and so taking farewell of the beggars I boarded the train for Rangoon. At Pyinmana Station I managed to lift the wallet of a man who was fast asleep. The wallet contained K 720/- and I went into town to buy a bedroll and some new clothes for myself with the money. When I arrived in Rangoon the following day I went directly to the foreshore and boarded the steamer for Maubin.

In Maubin I spent the night at my grandmother's house, and the next day sent word of my arrival to Kanyinwa, a village 8 miles away where my aunt lived. Two cousins of mine came for me by dugout canoe. They appeared to be very poor and so I took them into town and fitted them out in new clothes. I also bought a great quantity of provisions for my aunt in the village. We then left for Kayinwa at 2 p.m. arriving in the village only at 7 o'clock that night.

My aunt had fallen on hard times. Formerly her family had owned over 100 acres of land and 10 yoke of oxen and had lived in a spacious wooden bungalow. Now they were reduced to living in a small thatch hut and had lost everything except one small cow against which they had borrowed 100 kyats. My aunt wept when she told me all this.

The people in the village were living in wretched poverty.

They had just one set of clothing each, that which they had on at the moment. They could not afford cooking oil and had to bake the fish they caught from the river. They were so poor that they did not even have enough money to buy a few peppers with which to season their food.

I felt extremely sorry for them all, and sent to Maubin for some extra provisions to be distributed among the most needy families in the village. I also paid off the debt on my aunt's cow and led it back to her. At the end of one month I had gone through all my money with the exception of 30 kyats, and so I said farewell to the village and returned to Rangoon.

From Rangoon I went on to Pegu, arriving in time for the Pegu Pagoda Festival. Pickpockets and thieves from all over the country had congregated at this festival in anticipation of easy picking among the holiday crowd. The police determined to forestall them had rounded up 800 known petty criminals for detention until the end of the festival. Luckily I was not included in the group.

On the first night I managed to detach a gold necklace from a sleeping woman and a gold ring from a man. The next night I stole a gem necklace and the following day a pair of children's earrings. After lifting a gold necklace from a child the next day I left Pegu and went up-country to Meiktila, Kyawkse, Mandalay and Maymyo.

At Maymyo I heard of the Bawgyo Pagoda Festival to be held shortly at Hsipaw and made my way there. This annual festival was the occasion for much gambling, and I struck up an acquaintance with the proprietor of a gambling booth. This man offered me a job as his assistant and I gladly accepted. Twelve days later the festival ended, and I left with wages amounting to one hundred kyats in my pocket.

From Hsipaw I went on to Mandalay, Meiktila and Myingyan, where I lost all my money except 10 kyats in a gambling den. At the Panaing pagoda festival I managed to steal a wallet containing K 370/- from a man who was fast asleep and a watch from another person. For the next year or so I toured the whole of Upper Burma, visiting all the pagoda festivals in turn and setting up gambling booths, while at the time keeping my eyes skinned for a chance to steal anything worthwhile. In spite of several close shaves with the police I was never caught red handed.

Strangely enough my eventual arrest had nothing to do with

any of my previous crimes. I had returned to Rangoon and had taken to sleeping on the Pagoda Road Station platform. After three nights or so a police patrol from the Cantoment Police Precinct inspected the railway station and found me sleeping on a bench. I was taken into custody, together with a boy named A-Hussein, and sent here for detention pending trial. Although I have been here forty days my case has not yet come up for hearing. I hear that A-Hussein is not quite right in the head, and that the delay is due to his inability to appear in court.

I have no plans as to what I shall do when I get out. I have lived my life as I saw fit and I shall continue to do so when I am released.

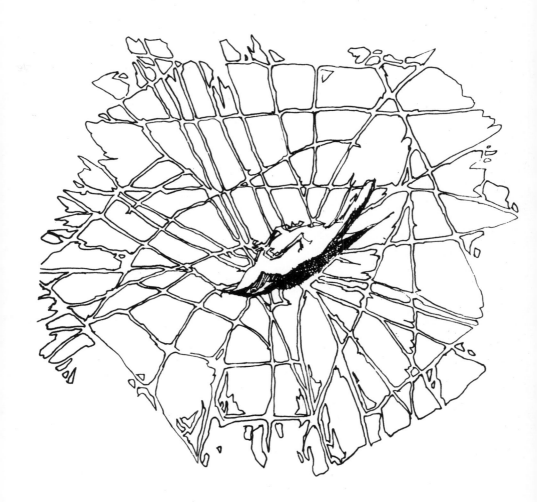

IX
THE STRAY BIRD

Homosexual prisoners are kept strictly segregated from ordinary prisoners in the Rangoon Central Jail. Permission has to be obtained from the authorities just to enter their compound, and it is no easy matter to get such permission. This group is well represented in the prison population, and as a group cannot be lightly dismissed. They are the cause of frequent breakings, knifings and murders among the other prisoners. The prison authorities often complain, declaring that they would much rather control a hundred ordinary convicts than one homosexual.

Homosexuality constitutes an ever recurring problem in the prisons. As an observer of prison life I could not afford to ignore the issue, but how was I to go about getting an interview with one of them? It would not do for me to be seen visiting their quarters and if they appeared at all outside their enclosure they were immediately subjected to the most blatant sexual advances, with the result that the authorities had forbidden them to leave their quarters altogether. In spite of these difficulties, however, I managed to persuade them to allow a young homosexual prisoner named Maung Than Way to visit me in our dormitory to be interviewed.

Maung Than Way was an amiable young man of slight build and somewhat sallow complexion. When he appeared for the interview he had on a tattered shirt and a longyi which was fastened so as to resemble a woman's skirt.

When the prisoner who had gone to fetch him told Maung Than Way that Ludu U Hla had sent for him, the boy realised at once the matters on which I wished to question him and confided to the messenger that he was fully prepared to tell me all that I wanted to know, if it would only help other young people to escape the fate that had befallen him.

The following is the pathetic story of Maung Than Way as related to the author.

*

I came from the Lethamadan quarter near the Shwe-pyaung-pyaung pagoda in Henzada town, but I was born in Kyon-pyaw. My parents were U Htun Maung and Daw Khin Kyi. I have two sisters.

When the Japanese Army entered Burma I was just four or five years old, and we spent the entire period of the occupation in Kyonpyaw. My parents traded in dry goods such as dried fish and chillies, while my sisters manufactured cheroots for a living. After the British reoccupied Burma we moved to Henzada. When things became settled, my father began travelling up-country by boat, carrying rice to places like Pakokku and Myingyan, and bringing back cooking oil and tobacco for sale in the Delta.

I was enrolled at the age of eight in the Henzada National School and studied there till I passed the Fifth Standard. The Headmaster was U Myint Soe. When I was seven I was novitiated into the Buddhist religion at the Withudda Monastery after which I stayed in the monastery for three weeks, receiving religious instruction.

In 1948, when insurrections broke out we moved to Rangoon, where we built a hut of our own in the Wa Wa Win area off Prome Road on the site of the present Reviewing Stand. By this time my parents were too old to work. My sisters continued making cheroots while I got a job at the Triple Five Canvas Shoe Factory. My sisters earned two to two and a half kyats a day, while I made kyats 2.50. Transport to and from the factory cost half a kyat. I could not afford to go home for lunch, and so I took a lunch box with me to work.

In 1953 the Reviewing Stand was constructed and the whole neighbourhood was demolished. However everyone received compensation and we were given K 100/- for our little hut.

About three months before we moved my father fell sick and died. Two months later my mother was bitten by a mad dog. At first we did not realise that the dog was rabid. Even when mother fell sick we thought that it was just an ordinary fever which she had contracted. When we finally realised the truth we took her to the monastery where the monk administered medicine to her. She became violent and tried to bite and scratch us and was subdued with great difficulty. We then took her to the Hospital, in the hope that they might be able to cure her, but they examined her and declared that it was too late to save her. We brought her back home, but she expired in the ambulance.

A year after we arrived in Rangoon the younger of my two sisters got married and her husband moved in with us. The elder sister remained single.

When we were evicted from the Wa Wa Win Quarter we moved to Kamayut, because of the lower land revenue rates prevailing there. My brother-in-law worked as a bus conductor on the Insein Bus Line for a salary of ninety kyats a month.

As playmates I had only my two sisters when I was young. Being the youngest I was spoiled by everyone and especially by my sisters, who would dress me up in their clothes for fun. Almost without knowing it I was gradually becoming a homosexual.

My sister's husband disapproved of my effeminacy from the start. To him I was a man, and he felt that I ought to shoulder a man's responsibilities. Gradually my sisters came round to his view and we began to have many quarrels on the subject. Finally they declared that so long as I refused to change my ways I would be unwelcome in their house and drove me out.

Before long I had drifted into the company of others like me, and I was soon frequenting the area in the centre of the city near Bandoola Park, the Sule Pagoda Roundabout and Pansodan in the company of three or four transvestites. This area was the regular beat of forty to fifty homosexuals of various races, colour and creeds. Some were chinese, some Sardees, some Anglo-Burmese, and some Anglo-Indian. They had all congregated in this area, some even coming from distant places like Arakan, Ye, Merqui, Tavoy, Mandalay, Meiktila, Myitkyina and Bhamo. Every evening they would dress up in their finest feminine apparel, primp themselves up and parade mincingly up and down the streets. There was a lot of jealousy among them, and they would vie with one another to see who looked the prettiest. I was the poorest and sorriest looking of the lot.

When I arrived, the others looked askance at me, as a flock of birds will look at a newcomer that has strayed into their midst. However, when I related my story the Vice-President of their society

Ma Sein, and another homosexual named Than Tin Gyi took pity on me and took me to a place near the Win Win Cinema in Pansodan to see their President, Sein Ma Ma. There was only one other transvestite more powerful than Sein Ma Ma, and that was the wealthy Ashar Gyan.

Sein Ma Ma Gyi greeted me warmly, saying "Come, come, daughter and made me feel welcome. He questioned me closely and then commented that I was still very green and inexperienced. He further detailed another transvestite to act as my instructor. This was a person of about my own age, but of a fairer complexion. He was the son of an engineer who lived near the football grounds in Syriam, and was variously called Miss Sule, Frontier Queen, Sein Nyunt, and Awin.

Under Awins tutelage I quickly learned the art of coquetry and how to please a man in bed. I was also dressed up in pretty clothes and properly cared for by Sein Ma Ma Gyi. Before long I was put to work as a prostitute. I do not have any idea of how much money was paid for my services. I only know that I was enjoying the life. There were others who were not as brazen as we were about our feelings. They were those homosexuals who secretly indulged their tastes by coming to our houses and submitting to the male clients.

I know that wealthy Indians tended to pay very good fees for our services. Like women prostitutes we would sometimes be "hired out " on order and on those occasions we were taken by car either to private houses or to places like the Inya lakes.

After about six months of this kind of life I found that I had contracted syphilis. I gained admission to the Rangoon General Hospital with the help of an Assitant Surgeon who happened to be a homosexual too, and was hospitalized for two months before I was discharged as cured. When I returned home, Sein Ma Ma gave me a full set of jewellery, all my clothes, my bed-roll, and kyat 500/- in cash and drove me from the house.

Upon leaving Sein Ma Ma I moved in with a trishawman who lived in Boundary Road. Within three months all my money was gone, and the trishawman too then drove me out. I was forced to strike out on my own, using the womanly wiles that I had been taught by Sein Nyunt alias Awin.

I began to walk the streets around Bandoola Park and the

Sule Traffic Circle. However even my utmost efforts did not bring in more than two kyats a day and so I began to pickpocket as well. When I was fortunate enough to lift a fat wallet, I would select a man of my choice and pay him to spend a few nights of pleasure with me. When my money was exhausted the man would leave me, sad and embittered at my fate and I was forced to revert to prostitution and stealing.

On March 27th 1954, which was Resistance Day a well dressed man with a strong Arakanese accent took me along to the Inya Lake side, saying I resembled his wife and that he would pay me well if I would let him have sexual relations with me. I noticed three hundred kyat notes and a Parker fountain pen in his pocket. While he was having his pleasure I quietly transferred them to my person. He did not appear to notice anything and we parted company amicably. However, on my way home, the bus on which I was travelling was stopped, and this man climbed aboard. He accused me of the theft, saying that I had been following him around and must have extracted three hundred kyats and a fountain pen from his pocket. When they searched me they naturally found the items on me, where upon he hit me in the face and hauled me off the police station, where a case was opened against me under Section 379 of the Penal Code.

On March 29th I entered Rangoon Central Jail with handcuffs on my wrists. I was so frightened that I could not control the trembling in my body. Some took pity on me, but others wanted to ridicule me.

For this first offense I was given a sentence of four months. I was placed on the upper floor of Cell Block No. 6. I did not realise at first that there were sex maniacs in that dormitory, but I soon found out. Up to seven or eight of these other prisoners gave me no rest either by night or by day, until finally I could stand it no longer and appealed to the Deputy Warden. On August 29th I was transferred to the homosexuals' Compound. Only then was I allowed to live in peace.

When I was released from jail I returned to Bandoola Park and carried on where I had left off. Three weeks later I was caught having sexual relations with a man and arrested together with my mentor Awin and one other and charged under Section 3-1 (a) (1).

We were found guilty and I was sentenced to five months in jail. Awin elected to take twenty lashes instead, knowing that as a homosexual she would not be beaten severely.

In prison I became the mistress of a senior prison official. Ten days after my release I was back in prison for a seven day sentence for ticketless travel on a train. Again I had to live with the same official. My present term of imprisonment is the fourth also for homosexual practices.

When I am set free I shall have to continue following the same profession as before. My sisters will not take me in, and whenever I appear they drive me away with blows and curses. They will not even give me a cup of water to drink.

*

When I interviewed him in 1955 Maung Than Way was only twenty two years old. There was an unhealthy pallor on his face and he had evidently lost much weight, and it was apparent that the prison was no "rest camp" for him where he could rebuild his energies and regain his health.

X
THE OPIUM SMUGGLER

How was it possible that such a slim and delicately formed youth had ended up in this harsh forbidding prison? When I first met Maung Nyein in Rangoon Central Jail he had just turned seventeen. Had he lied regarding his age to the authorities because he had not wanted to be sent to the Boys' Reformatory? When I learned that he was from Mandalay and that he used to live near the Eindawgar Pagoda I became even more interested in getting his story. Perhaps he was a neighbour of my good friend U Tha Htoo, who lived in that neighbourhood. When I approached the boy he readily consented to relate to me his experiences. The following is his account :

*

I was born in a house near the north entrance to the Eindawyar Pagoda. My father is U Ant Bwai and my mother Ma Shwe Hnit. They earned a living by running a small tailoring shop.

I am the youngest of seven brothers and sisters. When I was six years old I was enrolled in Upannawa's Thayet-taw Monastery school in Sagaing, where I learnt the Buddhist scriptures and the alphabet and picked up some rudiments of arithmetic as well. I studied there till I was eight years of age. My brothers stayed with my parents in Mandalay and did not attend the monastic school.

I had been drawn to the monk Upannawa when he was studying at the Mandalay Masoyein Monastery, when he had regularly come to our house for almsfood. When he returned to his Sagaing retreat I had followed him there without informing my parents of my intentions. I have not set eyes on my parents since then. I wrote to them once or twice from Rangoon, but did not enclose my correct address.

As far as I can remember, the Thayet-taw Monsatery was a

teaching monastery housing many monks, novices and students. When the monks went on their rounds for almsfood we boys had to look after the monastery. There was a boy from the Shwebo area named Thein Dan who was fourteen or fifteen years old and senior to us in the school. He would not eat with us, paying for his meals at the Nunnery instead. However he had to come and sleep with us. Being much older and bigger than us he would often take away our best clothes for himself, order us around and generally play the bully.

One day I had a violent quarrel with him, and seizing a long knife I hacked at his head. Instead of hitting his head squarely the sword hit it a glancing blow, slicing off his right ear and making a deep cut in his shoulder. Gathering my few personal belongings I fled, taking with me the two hundred kyats entrusted to me by Upannawa and another monk U Sandimar to buy necessities on their behalf, they being monks and as such prohibited from handling money themselves.

At first I ran away to the Shwebo area, making my way to Hsadaung to the house of an acquaintance of mine. I stayed with him for four or five months, and then took a train back to Mandalay. When I arrived in Mandalay I did not look up my folks, but slept at the Railway Station instead. At that time I was nine years old.

The two hundred kyats I had brought with me had been almost all spent, but my friend Hla Myint from Hsadaung had given me fifty kyats for expenses. My one desire being to visit the great city of Rangoon of which I had heard so much, I boarded the next Rangoon bound train. Trying to conserve my money as much as possible I travelled without a ticket.

On the train I struck up an acquaintanceship with a Ko Thein Aung from Ma-u-gon in Rangoon. At every stop I would eagerly ask him the name of the station and how far we were still from the capital city.

Ko Thein Aung had his wife and family with him, and they took pity on me and urged me to come along and stay with them in Ma-u-gon. Since I had nowhere else to go I gladly accepted their kind offer.

Ko Thein Aung was a mechanic on a motor launch plying between Rangoon and Tavoy. While living with him I helped him in the disposal of goods brought to Rangoon on his launch, and was paid at the rate of K 2.50 for every hundred kyats worth of goods moved. I handed over all my earnings to Ko Thein Aung, and he would buy clothes and other necessities for me out of that money. I stayed with Ko Thein Aung and his family for nearly two years.

While working for Ko Thein Aung I had become friendly with all the traders from Mergui, Tavoy and Moulmein with the result that the various trading houses were glad to have my services as go-between between them and the traders. One day Daw Than Tin the proprietress of the Win Win Trading house near the Central Bazaar on Pagoda Road asked me to come and work for her. With the consent of Ko Thein Aung she adopted me as her son.

My work with Daw Than Tin consisted of going to the Botataung and Keighly Street jetties and the Railway warehouses and taking delivery of the goods sent from the districts to her trading house, and to drum up new custom for her firm from among the traders. I also had to collect payments on her behalf from merchants in Theingyi Market and Yebaw Market.

One day, when making the rounds to collect this money a shopkeeper requested me to wait for an hour or so, while they got together the amount owed to us. Accordingly I went to a tea shop and stayed there until 4 p.m. at which time I returned to the shop.

It was only when I reached his shop that I realised that I had left the money that I had already collected together with all the account books, at the teashop. I hurriedly retraced my steps, but found that I was too late and that the money and the books were gone.

Not daring to face my foster mother after this, I took a bus for Kyaiksagaing Village near Taikkyi. I had managed to save five hundred kyats which I had entrusted to a the owner of a Chinese restaurant and I used this money for expenses. I introduced myself to a man named Ko Ye Myint, pretending that I had come to the neighbourhood to buy duck eggs in bulk, and obtained his permission to sleep in his house. During the day I would leave for Hmawbi where I would roam about aimlessly, returning only at night to the village. I spent 10 days in this fashion. At the end of which I moved to Taikkyi. Fifteen days later I returned to Rangoon to Ko Thein Aung's house.

Ko Thein Aung was away on a trip to Tavoy, but came back after about fifteen days. Before he came home he had encountered my foster mother who had made a full report to him about my conduct, and when he entered the house he was in a towering rage.

However when I explained the circumstances under which I had absconded he grew calmer and went to my foster mother and recounted my version of the affair to her. She wept when she heard of my experiences and came to the house to try and persuade me to come back to her. I did not want to go with her, but Ko Thein Aung added his voice to her entreaties and so finally I gave in and accompanied her home.

Once back at her house I resumed my duties at the agency. I also enrolled for night school where I was taught English for a tuition fee of ten kyats a month. I was fourteen years old at the time. After some five months or so, I gave a love letter to a girl student and she promptly went and informed the schoolteacher. Fearing that the teacher would report the matter to my foster mother, I ran away again from home. I made my way to Kyaiksagaing near Taikkyi and stayed there for three days. After which I went home. My foster mother had reported my disappearance to the police and was overjoyed to see me. I continued working for her during the daytime, but refused to attend any more evening classes.

Among the clients at the trading house were two middle-aged ladies from Moulmein. These ladies traded in durian and mangosteen fruit, but they also dealt in a more sinister commodity, namely opium, and they enlisted my aid in their activities. I was paid well for my services and saw no reason why I should not earn some easy money, but I took good case not to let my foster mother know of what was going on under her very nose.

These ladies made arrangements for the purchase of opium from a trading house in Phongyi Street. My job was to take the consignments of opium and deliver them to motorised fishing boats bound for Moulmein. The ladies would precede me either by train or by plane and take delivery of the goods upon their arrival. For every ball of opium transported in this way I was given ten kyats.

Very soon however, these women began to default on their payments, until they owed me a total of almost three hundred kyats. One day they entrusted me with the sum of 800/- kyats for delivery to the Phongyi Street trading house. I told them jokingly that I would deduct the money they owed me from the eight hundred kyats, but they threatened to report me to the police if I dared to do so.

I was burning with resentment, and there and then decided to keep the money. I left them ostensibly to go to Phongyi Street, and after a while I returned, pretending that I had made the necessary payment. I left the house again, telling them that I was going to the movies. I did actually see a movie-show, but afterwards I made my way to a friend's house in Sangyaung and moved in with him. Two days later I heard that the two ladies had gone to the police-station and lodged a complaint against me for misappropriation. I left for Taikkyi, where I stayed for twelve days, at the end of which I returned to Rangoon where I found a job in a tea-shop in Ma-U-Gon.

A friend from a bar on Pagoda Road named Ko Mutta found out where I was working and persuaded me to give myself up to the police, assuring me that he would come and bail me out immediately. I agreed, and the next day police from the Pabedan Station came and arrested me. The next day was a Sunday and all offices were closed. Ko Mutta did not appear and I was sent to the Rangoon Central Jail.

I have been here for five months now. My foster mother must have believed all that the two women told her. At my trial I tried to explain that the money I had taken was money that they owed me for helping them in their opium dealing. They insisted that I had stolen the money and my foster-mother testified that I did not have any money coming to me. I had no money to pay a lawyer and no one to back up my story. On 11-7-55 I was sentenced to one year's rigorous imprisonment.

When I am released I will join a friend who is at present still in this prison, but who will be released in October. He is serving a sentence of six months for being found in possession of a dagger on his person. He is going to rejoin his mother, but has promised to wait for me.

I have no intention whatsoever of returning to Mandalay. I have news that both my parents are dead. My brothers and sisters may be still living, but of that I am not sure.

*

I wish I had news of Maung Nyein to give his relatives but I have heard nothing of him since his release from prison. All I know is that up till 1956 he had still not been readmitted to the Rangoon Central Jail.

XI
THE SOLDIER

The short fair prisoner of medium build whom I was interviewing gave his name as Maung Soe Win, Although he claimed to be 21 years old, to me he looked no older than 18. This Kayah youth should never have been imprisoned in the first place. His story is given below in his own words.

*

My father originally came from Salin and my mother from In-paw-khon in Yaung-Shwe. Father worked as a peon in the Public Works Department at Loilem. My parents had four children but only two are still living. My elder sister is married and gone to live with her husband. Mother died in 1947 when I was thirteen years old.

When I reached the age of six I was enrolled in the Anglo-Vernacular School at Loilem and studied there up to the Second Standard. I then transferred to a secondary school where I studied up till the Fifth Standard. In 1947 I left school, in part because my mother's death had affected me greatly. Mother had opened a restaurant before she died, and had been liberal with credit for the customers. She also freely gave loans to many acquaintances. When mother died these debtors refused to acknowledge their debts and the loans had to be written off. We finally had to   sell both the restaurant and our house. I was greatly upset because of these things, as my father also could no longer afford to send me to school, I had to cut short my education.

After leaving school I went to live with a friend named Kyaw Myint in Kyaukme-Namsahm who was working as an overseer. This friend trained me for a year and then got me a job as assistant overseer at a monthly salary of K 135/-. However being just seventeen at the time I began to miss my father badly and so after working for eighteen months I resigned from the position.

Father had also left his job and I was entered as an apprentice in my sister's tailoring shop for six months. Only at the end of this period was I employed in the shop as a paid worker.

One day my friends came to tell me of an Army Recruitment poster which they had seen in town. I went along with them to take a look at the poster, and found that it listed the salary, rations, uniform and equipment which would be issued to each recruit upon enlistment giving the monetary value of each item. The total seemed an enormous sum to me.

My friends wanted to join up, and urged me to do likewise. At that time the young men in our town were very keen on enlisting in the Army, because of the Kuomintang incursions into the Loilem District, and we felt it our duty to take up arms to repel the invaders. Furthermore we felt that without arms we would be helpless in case the Chinese took Loilem and it would be far more honourable to die fighting with weapons in our hands, and so all of us signed up straight away.

When I got home my brother-in-law upbraided me for what I had done. He pointed out that a soldier's lot was a very hard one, and I would have a very difficult time in the Army. He himself had served as a soldier during the British regime and he knew the hardships I would have to undergo. He tried to dissuade me from reporting for duty, but I was determined to fight the Kuomintang enemy and on January 8, 1953 I presented myself at the induction centre and was brought to Loilem.

The outfit I joined was the First Kayah Rifles, then in process of formation and intended to replace the Karenni irregulars stationed in Kayah State. There were eighty-two recruits from Loikaw and after a period of twenty days we were all sent to Kalaw to await the arrival of twenty-nine others. In Kalaw we were attached to the Twenty-First Light Infantry.

The Kayah Rifles had already distinguished themselves in action against the enemy and after heavy fighting had managed to defeat them in the field. The First Kayah had been then ordered to Myitkyina, where we were sent to join these victorious troops.

At Myitkyina our equipment was issued to us and we were put through a four months course of basic military training. We were then sent out on fighting patrols in the Sadon Hsama area. Near Sadon village we captured twelve Chinese soldiers from the Kuomintang Army who had come to exact tribute from the villagers. We sent the prisoners to Myitkyina from where they were sent on to Mandalay. After three months in the field we were recalled to Myitkyina and sent to rejoin our respective companies.

In Myitkyina I was assigned the task of training new recruits even though I was still a private myself. I was also sent to Mandalay together with another soldier to buy materials for the Buddhist Novitiation Ceremony held by the Battalion.

One day six of us from the unit took fifteen days leave, leaving Myitkyina together. My comrades proceeded to the Shan States to visit relatives while I decided to go to Rangoon, having never been there in my whole life.

While in Rangoon I went to see a friend who lived in Mingaladon. On the return trip, to the city I just barely managed to catch the train. Having had to run to board the train I did not have any time to buy a ticket. Twenty minutes after the train left the station, the conductor came along, and finding that I had no ticket put me under arrest, brushing aside all my attempts at explanation. A thirteen year old boy in the same carriage was also arrested.

On 10-8-55 I was brought before a magistrate. I submitted that I was a soldier, and that my paybook and other papers could be found in the house near Baluma Market where I was staying. In spite of this my occupation was listed as "coolie". Without even bothering to question me the magistrate passed judgement that I was to pay a fine of fifteen kyats or in lieu of that serve a sentence of fifteen days in prison. He seemed bored by the whole affair.

I wrote a note to my host in the Baluma Market house asking him to send fifteen kyats of my money to enable me to pay the fine, and entrusted it for delivery to a police constable in the court, but he merely took the note and omitted to deliver it. In this way I found myself unexpectedly in prison.

Ever since my sister died during an Allied bombing raid during the war I have been dogged by ill fortune, Then mother died and I had to give up my education. She had been preparing to send me to attend St. Peter's Mission High School in Mandalay, but all arrangements had to be cancelled on her death. And now I have become a convict with a prison record.

I do not mix much with the other prisoners. On return from work I usually turn in early. Their conversation holds no interest for me. I shall be here only for fifteen days, but if I get involved with the wrong company I may find myself in prison again for a much longer period.

When one of their number is about to be released the prisoners call out to him. "Come and pay us a visit sometime. Board a train without buying a ticket. That should do it." They all know that this is the quickest way to get yourself in prison and out again in next to no time. They joke about it among themselves, but to an honest person like me even a short prison sentence is no laughing matter.

I have already overstayed my leave and I do not know whether I shall be punished for this also. I hope the army authorities will take into consideration my previous spotless record and treat me leninently. If they should find out that I have been in jail they may decide to stop all future promotions for me. I do not know what to do.

My host in Rangoon is Ko Aung Bo, the brother of Sergeant-Clerk Ko Aung Pe from our unit. He has no way of knowing my whereabouts and must be wordering what has happened to me. As soon as I am released I must go to see him at once. He must be very worried by now.

XII
THE ORPHAN

Among the many young inmates of Rangoon Central Jail, Maung Chit Tin appeared to be the youngest. He was a quick and alert child and I surmised that he had become so by having had to live on his wits from an early age, having been orphaned when very young. He could not even recall the death of his parents. He was reluctant to tell me his story and broke down and wept. We tried to stop his tears as best as we could and after he had composed himself this was the story that he related.

*

My father was Ko Ba Tin and my mother Ma Hnin Sein. They lived in Pegu near the Shwetharlyaung Pagoda. They sold Burmese rice cakes for a living. Both of them passed away while I was still an infant and I was adopted by Ko Po Ohn and Ma Kyi Aung. I have one elder brother and one elder sister. My original parents were Indian Muslims and so my brother was called "Pathan" by one and all.

I was first enrolled in the Hpaung-daw-U school in Pegu. I was a poor scholar and was often caned for not applying myself to my studies. This led to my playing truant as often as possible, with the result that I learned little more than the letters of the alphabet. Finally I stole a train ride to Rangoon, where I eked out a living by filching things from shops and people. I had no fixed place of abode, but slept wherever I could find shelter, which was usually near the cinema halls. My brother had run away to Rangoon about a year before me, but I was unable to trace him.

When I was eight years old I was caught stealing in front of the Continental Confectionary in Rangoon. I was sent to the Boy's Reformatory on Boundary Road. Security was very strict here and there was no way in which one could escape. We were given a set of clothing to wear in the institution. On special occasions when visitors were expected we were fitted out in new clothes. Our duties consisted mainly of gardening, drawing water and washing clothes.

There were about one hundred inmates in the school at that time. We had to rise at 6 a.m. and do calisthenics. Then from 7 a.m. to 10 a.m. we had to attend classes. At 10 o'clock we were given our morning meal consisting usually of rice and vegetable curry. After that meal we had to clean up.

In the afternoon we had to work in the garden. Dinner was set at 5 p.m. At 7 we had evening prayers. Although we had boys of many different races and creeds we all had to recite the Buddhist scriptures. Lights-out was at eight o'clock.

The children were taught Burmese, English, Arithmetic and Geography in the reformatory. After five years in this school I had learned to read and write. (Upon being tested, the prisoner could read newspaper headlines but haltingly and could not read certain combination of letters at all - Author)

All of our bathing had to be done in the small pond where clothes and dirty plates and pots and pans were washed. It was no wonder that all of us had lice and other vermin as well as ugly mud-sores on our bodies. For washing laundry we were given only six bars of soap for every 100 items of clothing.

Eventually I was appointed a monitor to supervise the work of the other boys. In 1955, during the Water Festival I was detailed to draw water from the pond outside the school with two other boys named Sein Hlaing and Abdul Karim. We took this opportunity to escape. Sein Hlaing went back to his sister and Abdul Karim crossed the river to Dallah to rejoin his sister.

I had no relatives with whom to take shelter and so I struck up an acquaintance with a boy a little older than me, named Kyaw Win. We would wander around during the day and at night climb onto the flat-roofs of the buildings on Moghul Street and sleep there. Two months later I was apprehended near the Cinema Halls on Sule Pagoda Road by officers from the Boy's Home.

Upon being returned to Boundary Road, I was given fifty lashes with the cane. This was to discourage other would be truants. This was standard procedure for a first offender. For a second offense the punishment was a hundred strokes. In addition to this beating I had my head shaven and was placed in solitary confinement and fed only after everyone else had eaten.

A month after my return the whole institute shifted to new premises near the Kabar Aye Pagoda. Our new quarters were bigger and better and the grounds were more spacious. There were also fields for cultivation attached to the School. Here we were taught trades such as tailoring and hairdressing. A few students were taught automobile repair and maintenance. Pupils in the fifth and sixth grades who showed scholastic promise were permitted to attend school outside the institution. The number of deliquent boys in the Reformatory was also increased.

In the year 1318 of the Burmese Era on the 2500th Anniversary of the founding of Buddhism, widespread celebrations were held and our school participated in the festivities. Three or four days after the festival I ran away again from the institution. Crossing the Chinese lady's garden on the east side of the school at four in the afternoon, I caught a White Elephant Line bus and reached Moghul Street.

Luckily I ran into my brother "Pathan" that very night. From that time on I would not be parted from him. Pathan had had a variety of experiences since he had run away from home. He had worked at a great many occupations and visited all sorts of places. He had also served a term in the Boy's Reformatory and the police had their eye on him. He was nineteen years old at that time and was already married. He had brought his wife to live with our sister. (Pathan refused to relate all his experiences even to his brother saying that it would hurt him if the full story came out. - Author.)

During the day we would attend the cinema shows at the Jamal, Win Win and nearby cinema halls and at night we would break into and ransack the various houses in the neighbourhood. We would reconnoitre the area for a house with an open window and when we found one we would climb up usually by a waterpipe and help ourselves to wristwatches, jewelry and any other valuables that we could lay our hands on. After making a haul we would have a feast at an Indian restaurant and go on a spending spree.

For a long time we went undetected by the police. However, one day we happened to quarrel with a fellow named Gaung Pya and he must have given information against us, because the next morning at about 6 a.m., when we were burgling a shop selling steel trunks the police surrounded the shop and ordered us to come out. They called us by name. "Chit Tin, Pathan Lay, Kyaw Win, Charteik. "Come on out," they shouted. We did not obey, but instead tried to hide. Finally they entered and took us prisoners after giving each of us a severe beating. Kyaw Win received the greatest injuries. I was hit once and kicked once in the small of the back.

We were taken first to Pabedan Police Station. At three o'clock in the afternoon we were transferred to Central Lock-up on Bar Street. The next morning we were brought before a magistrate and charged under Section 447: Criminal Trespass. I was sent to the City Central Jail in June 1956 and this is why you find me here.

In the prison, young inmates like us are segregated like the homosexual prisoners. We are housed in the hospital building near the homosexual quarters. One of them, Asein, has adopted me and takes good care of me.

You ask me what I intend to do when I am released. I will give you a frank answer: I intend to continue stealing as before.

*

Two months later hearings on the case were held before the trial magistrate and Charteik Lay, Chit Tin and the other accused were discharged. A week later, on 14-9-56 the brothers Pathan and Maung Chit Tin were again caught breaking into a house on Moghul Street and sentenced to one month's imprisonment and readmitted to the Central Jail.

After serving their time they were again released. One wonders when they will be back. Will they be beaten up when apprehended and enter the prison with broken heads? Or will they be imprisoned for more serious offences than hitherto.

Maung Chit Tin is still a child. His statement that he is seventeen years old is likely to be false and made solely to escape being returned to the Boy's Reformatory. To my mind, he can hardly be a day older than fifteen.

XIII
THE BICYCLE THIEF

Tall and fair, and sporting a fashionable hair-cut, this youth could easily have been mistaken for a movie actor or a college student. He was a 19 year old Sino-Burman named Maung Sein Win. In addressing his elders he was always properly respectful but in his relations with his peers he could be stern and forbidding on occasion.

While he was serving his third term of imprisonment I approached him one day and asked him to relate to me the story of his life. This is what he had to say.

*

I was born in the town of Thongwa in Hanthawaddy District. My father was U Shu Wan, also called U Bar Bar. My mother is Daw Than Khin. I am the third of four children.

My elder brother at present runs his own general store in Thongwa. My elder sister is married, and my younger brother drives a motor vehicle in Rangoon.

Before the War my father worked as a clerk in a motor company on Pansodan. When the Japanese invaded Burma we fled to China by way of Lashio, Wanteing, and Kunming, China. My father managed to get a job in the Shin Wei Yin Han Motor Company, which was the parent company of the branch company on Pansodan. While we were in Kunming the Japanese bombed the city and so we took refuge in the countryside. A month later my father died. The motor company continued to provide us with living accomodation, rations, and a stipend for three whole years.

After the Japanese surrendered, the company sent us back to Burma. On the way back we had an accident near Pauk Shan and a passenger named Ma Kyi from Mandalay suffered a broken arm. Luckily, we escaped unscathed. On arrival in Rangoon we went to the

Kyaukmyaung neighbourhood to put up with my aunt who lived there. After a while we moved back to Thongwa. In Thongwa my mother married a widower with a 12 year old daughter. I was also 12 years old at that time.

Four months later we moved again to Rangoon. I did not get along with my stepfather, and went to stay with my sister in Mandalay Road. My sister enrolled me in the Nelson School on U Wisara Road. After 3 months my mother came and took me back to her home and had me transferred to Saya Kho's School. I studied for a year in Saya Kho's School, after which my stepfather forced me to give up my studies. I realised that it was impossible for me to continue living in his house, and not long after that ran away for good. My delinquency dates from this time.

The first night I spent sitting up all night rear Bogyoke Market in the company of flower girls and sellers of vegetable greens. The next night I helped out at an all-night tea-shop and was given dinner as payment. I worked there for five days, at the end of which I made the acquaintance of the notorious pickpocket Tin Myint, alias "Diamond". Tin Myint asked me where I came from, and when I replied that I had run away from home after quarreling with my stepfather, took me along to live with him and his young wife in their house on Morton Street.

For the first fifteen to twenty days I did not have to do anything in his house other than eat and rest. Then he spent four or five days in teaching me how to pick a lock. Shortly afterwards he was arrested and sentenced to 9 months imprisonment. There was no one left but me to support his young wife and at his urging I set out to earn some money.

He had left a skeleton key at home which could be used to open almost any make of bicycle lock. I began using the key to steal bicycles and sell them, turning over the proceeds to his wife.

Ten days after his release we tried to break into a house and were surprised in the act. Diamond escaped but I was caught. After spending a night at the Barr Street Police Station I was sent to "Mothers" Home near Inya Lake. I was 14 years old at the time, and this was my first offence.

I spent a total of 6 months at this Boys' Home. When I was discharged from the school I did not return to the house on Seventh

Street but instead went to stay with a friend who worked in an Indian Laundry on 38th Street. While living there I made another skeleton key and started stealing bicycles again. Two or three months later I was arrested and spent another 9 months in Jail. The authorities tried to have me readmitted to "Mother's Home, but she refused to accept me, and I was sent to the Rangoon Central Jail, instead.

On the expiry of my sentence I looked up bicycle thieves Tin Myint and Kyaung Lay whom I had met in prison, and moved in with them. From this time on I gave up bicycle stealing and began to concentrate on housebreaking. I would put a small jemmy in my bag and scout around for houses which were locked up, during the daytime. Most of my burglaries were carried out in the afternoon.

Things went on smoothly for a while until one day when I was ransacking the house of Member of Parliament U Than Tun in Yankin the members of the household returned home and I was caught red-handed. They did not ill-treat me in any way, merely handing me over to the police. Only when I arrived at the Thingangyun Police Station was I beaten up by the officers. A little while later I found myself back in Rangoon Central Jail.

The fifth Additional Magistrate sentenced me to 20 Lashes. After I was released I returned to the house on 29th Street in Kandawlay. Tin Myint and Kyaung Lay were still engaged in stealing bicycles. Neither of them had yet been arrested.

Three or four months later, officers from the Latter Street Police Station came and took me into custody and booked me on suspicion in a case of bicycle theft. However this was one occasion on which I was truly innocent and they had no other recourse but to release me a week later.

About a month after this incident eight bicycles were stolen from the Kyauktada precinct. This was the work of Kyaunglay. To add insult to injury he had taken the bicycles from the stand located right in front of Police Headquarters. We warned him of the risks he was running on spiriting the bicycles away from under the very noses of the police but could not dissuade him from making further attempts. On his next try the police were lying in wait for him and he was caught. When interrogated he implicated the two of us, and we were also taken into custody. We denied the charges but the Second Additional Magistrate found us guilty and sentenced us to fifteen Lashes each.

Kyaunggalay was not so fortunate. He was given a sentence of 18 months' rigorous imprisonment.

Three months later I succeeded in breaking into an Indian house rear the Hninzigon Maternity Home. Shortly afterwards I met an exconvict named Aye Kyi to whom I gave fifty kyats, with the one request that he refrain from calling me Sein Win in public, since I had accidentally dropped a prescription for medicine with my name on it at the scene of the crime.

Ten days later, while I was having tea in a shop near the Wizaya Cinema Hall on U Wizara Road, Aye Kyi appeared and called out to me: "Sein Win, Hey, Sein Win". There were some policemen sitting at a nearby table at the time and I pretended not to hear him but he came right up to my table, tapped me on the shoulder and said "Hey, Sein Win". The policemen immediately got to their feet and informed me that I was under arrest.

I spent two weeks in the police station, during which period I was regularly beaten and interrogated by the police. They demanded that I reveal all that I knew of any crimes that had been committed recently. I declined to play the informer, but freely confessed to my part in the burglary on the Indian house. The police were dissatisfied with this, but in the face of my steadfast refusal to implicate anybody else they had to send me up on this sole charge. The Fifth Additional Magistrate found me guilty and sentenced me to six months rigorous imprisonment and I was brought here to serve my sentence.

*

Maung Sein Win planned to return to Thongwa upon the expiry of his sentence, saying that he did not stand a fair chance in Rangoon. Shortly after my interviews with him had been concluded he obtained his release, but in next to no time he was back inside the walls of the Rangoon Central Jail.

During his brief sojourn outside he had rented a house in Kan-Dawlay and had pretended to have a job as head clerk in a government office. He would leave early in the morning and return home after office hours laden with files and official looking documents. In this manner he managed to get into the good graces of a young seamstress who lived next door and induced her to marry him. Only when Sein Win was arrested two months later for another burglary did the poor girl realise that her husband was not a government servant but a well known criminal.

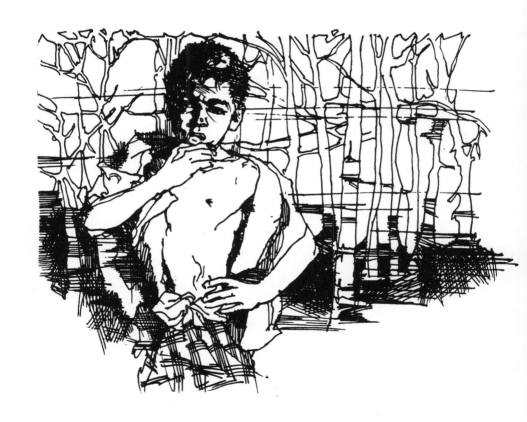

XIV
GIVE A DOG A BAD NAME

Kanniya the prisoner of Tamil extraction was the first born of Hindu parents. When he was born the midwife and the old woman in attendance had conducted nativity rites in which the umblical cord had been washed in a golden platter. Prayers for the sake of his future prosperity had been recited.

Kanniya was of unprepossing appearance. His parents were of Madras stock and his complexion was consequently rather dark. However, as if in compensation for his short stature and ugly face he posessed enormous strength. He would perform back-breaking tasks with ease and then ask if there was anything else he could do. In prison he would approach people and offer to do odd jobs for them.

He would launder my clothes for me and clean and tidy up my room. Occasionally he would dismantle my bed and wash it thoroughly to rid it of bed bugs.

He could read and write Hindi and would relate to me stories from the Hindu classics as he massaged me. An avid film-fan, he would retail the latest gossip concerning the stars of the Indian screen to me. On one occasion, when he saw me reading a book on Yoga and practising some of the postures and breathing exercises he was overcome with delight and at once squatted on the floor to demonstrate the proper technique.

When I asked him to tell me the story of his life he showed reluctance. "I don't want to tell you about myself Sahib" he said. "It is a very sad story. I don't think there is a single person in the whole world more unfortunate than me. Even Marx, Engels, Lenin or Mao Tse Tung could not have undergone the hardships that I have had to face." Upon being pressed further this is what he had to relate.

*

I was born in Mandalay. My father's name is Posa Lal Theva and my mother's Ramayi Amah. They are both of Tamil stock. They were married in India and then came to Mandalay where my father obtained a job as a clerk. He started betting on the horses and before long was deeply in debt both in Burma and India. After a while he had to return to India to face court action brought by creditors who were trying to recover their racing debts from him. I was left in Burma with my mother and a little sister four years younger than me.

My father left in 1938 and had not yet returned by 1939. Mother sold the house in Mandalay with all our belongings and moved to Rangoon where we had our relatives. In Rangoon we had great difficulty in making both ends meet. Mother had to sell off her jewelry piece by piece until she had none left. Finally she realised that she could not cope with the situation alone and in 1942 married a friend named Warhsu Devin who worked as a clerk in a butcher's shop at a salary of thirty-five kyats a month. Shortly after they married, my stepfather resigned from his job and set up business for himself as a butcher. Although he was a Hindu and as such would eat no beef himself, he nevertheless did not have any qualms concerning the slaughter of cows and the sale of their meat.

When he had saved about five thousand kyats he sold his business and opened a small gold-dealer's shop in Thingangyun. Around this time my mother gave birth to two more girls and one boy.

In 1945, when the British reoccupied the country, my step-father entered the city of Rangoon ahead of others and unlawfully occupied five apartments on Moghul Street. He also went into a partnership with four others and set up a gold-dealer's shop in Moghul Street in one of the apartments. He then sold one of the others for nine thousand kyats, another for ten thousand kyats and a third for twenty-five thousand kyats. In no time at all he had become a man of substance through dishonest means. He also bought out the other partners in the gold-dealer's business. However, although he made a lot of money he kept remitting most of it to India.

A lot of his prosperity was due to money-lending at usurious rates. He would charge interest at a monthly rate of ten per cent and whenever someone wanted a loan of a hundred kyats he would advance ten kyats in advance as interest for the first month and give the person only ninety kyats. This principal had to be repaid in daily instalments of three kyats. My job was to collect the daily payments from his debtors.

The Indian merchants who did business on Moghul Street usually sent diamonds and jewelry to India on ocean-going steamers plying between Rangoon and Indian ports. The ships' officers acted as couriers, the gems being packed in boxes of Cuticura Brand face powder. I remember seeing on one occasion the European captain of a ship being handed such a box. Other favourite places of concealment were false compartments in suitcases, hollow heels of European style shoes and handles of umbrellas and bicycles.

The quickest way to send money to Madras was to buy postal order permits from Indian labourers who had been granted permission to remit money to their families in India. Another method was to send an Indian labourer on an expense paid trip home. The steamer fare costs sixty kyats, and meals and other incidentals perhaps forty kyats more. Each passenger was permitted to take a bank draft for three hundred kyats and Burmese currency worth one hundred kyats. In addition a female passenger could take gold rings, gold bangles, earrings, necklaces and other items of jewelry with her. The Indian merchants in Rangoon would load down each labourer with the maximum permissible amount of jewelry and currency and send her to India, where she would be relieved of these by the merchant's agents and given a commission for her services.

Another method was to use the good offices of the authorities in the Banks. For every hundred kyats deposited with them they would remit seventy-five kyats to India and retain twenty-five kyats as their fee. I have never heard of anyone being arrested for these transactions.

Yet another method was to approach in Import Export Company. Suppose you had one hundred thousand kyats which you wished to remit to India. The company would give you a letter of credit for your money less twenty-five percent deducted as commission. You would send the letter to India where your agent would draw out the money. The Import-Export Company in its turn would use the hundred thousand kyats in Burmese currency to buy Burmese goods and export them to India to be sold for Indian rupees.

I am familiar with all these tricks used by Indian merchants because I have lived in close association with them over a period of many years.

*

In June 1947, my father Posa Lal Theva arrived in Rangoon from Madras on the S.S. Saralsa. After making enquiries as to our whereabouts he finally managed to trace us to Moghul Street. He appeared on the street one morning at about 9 a.m. and began walking up and down scanning the buildings with upturned face. My mother was on the front verandah of our fourth floor apartment at that time preparing the afternoon meal and their eyes met. She called out to me saying "Your father has come!" I immediately dashed out to the verandah and saw my father. "Father! Father!" I called out to him and he waved back. I ran back into the apartment intending to rush downstairs, but my mother had bolted the front door and stood with her back to it, refusing to permit me to leave. I heard my father calling "Kanniya, Kanniya my son, won't you please come down?" but I could not obey. After repeatedly calling my name he finally grew disheartened and went into a nearby restaurant to wait.

After a while when my mother went into the kitchen to cook lunch I quietly placed a chair in front of the door, undid the bolt and quickly ran downstairs and into the restaurant which I had seen my father enter. When I saw him I hurled myself into his arms and both of us wept for some time. Then he said to me "Son, Don't stay here. Come back with me to India." "Yes father," I replied. "I will come with you. I don't want to stay with stepfather. He ill-treats me so much." He then told me to go back to my mother for a while, saying that he would speak to my stepfather about letting me accompany him home. I was reluctant to do so, and told him that I would be beaten if I went back. However, at his urging I finally went home and sure enough was beaten soundly by my mother.

Father went to my stepfather and demanded the return of his son. My stepfather said that he was welcome to take both his children and good riddance. Father replied that as the father he was entitled to the male offspring while the mother was entitled to the female and that he would take only his son. My stepfather said that he would have to consult my wishes on the matter. He then sent word for me to come to the office and when I arrived asked me "Do you want to go along with your father, or would you like to remain with us?" "I want to go with father" I replied at once. He did not say anything but his demeanour showed that he did not like my answer. However, according to our customs, he gave me a wrist watch, earrings, a gold chain and gold rings worth about five hundred kyats in all and made me several suits as well.

When I returned to my mother to say goodbye she tried to get me to change my mind saying, "Don't go, my son. There is a famine in India and people are dying of starvation. You will not be able to get enough to eat. Stay here with us", but I was not to be moved. "I don't care" I told her "No matter what happens I intend to live with father. Stepfather beats me all the time and I am unhappy here."

On July 19th, 1947, General Aung San was assassinated and on July 20th we left for India on the S.S. Jalagoban. After a four day voyage we docked in Madras. A train journey lasting two nights brought us to my father's village of Pathupatay in Pathukothay District. When we arrived at my father's compound I saw that it contained two houses, and it was only then that I learned that my father had two wives in the village, and that he kept a wife in each of the two houses. He had three adolescent daughters and one young child.

Although my father owned some paddy land there was a drought that year and the yield of crops fell to one third that of normal. Everyone went hungry and the British authorities had to institute a strict system of rice rationing.

Since there was not enough rice to feed his two households my father started selling off my gold ornaments. My stepmothers would also pinch my cheeks hard occasionally saying "Your mother is rich. Why don't you go back to her?"

In this situation I had to depend on my wits to obtain enough food to eat. I first went to the younger of my father's wives and told her that the other wife was saying snide things about her and offered to report to her all that she said and did. I also ran errands for the second wife and wormed my way into her favour. In return she began to feed me properly.

Ten days later I went to the older women and repeated the same procedure, reporting all that the younger one had said about her. She in turn began to feed me well and to make much of me. In this fashion I alternated between my two stepmothers basking in the good graces of each in turn. Whenever one of them beat me I would report the matter to my father and he would immediately punish the offending wife. However, they usually managed to retaliate whenever my father's back was turned.

The famine in India grew worse day by day. In time I became a shadow of my former self, my ribs began sticking out of my body and my eyes became sunken in their sockets. I began to fear that I would starve to death. Finally I could stand it no longer and secretly wrote a letter to my mother explaining the situation to her, begging her forgiveness and asking to be taken back again. I did not even have the money to buy a stamp for the letter but posted it anyway.

When my mother received the letter she showed it to her husband and obtained his permission to come to Madras with her two children to fetch me. She did not come to the village but instead went to stay with my stepfather's relatives in the city. She then sent word by a messenger who came to me and said "Your mother has arrived and is asking for you. Come along with me." I immediately left with him, without even waiting to inform my father or his wives. We slept the night in a nearby town and the next day took a train trip to where my mother was waiting and we were finally reunited.

Two months later my father and his younger wife turned up. They had brought their own food packets with them, expecting no welcome especially in view of the food shortage, and my mother did not even invite them in. Instead she asked him truculently "What do you want?." Father replied "I have come to take my son back." At this my mother exploded in anger. She reviled him and called him all manner of names and shouted, "Look at the boy! Are you planning to kill him once and for all?" Father listened in silence for a while and then left for his village with my stepmother.

One month later when arrangements were being made for us to return to Burma it was discovered that my passport had been left behind in my father's house. Mother gave me the train fare and sent me to fetch the passport. When I arrived at my father's village he said to me "Son, don't go back. Stay here with me. If you live with that whore you will come to no good." When I told him that I was determined to accompany my mother back to Burma, he refused to let me have my passport and when I made to leave anyway, he and his wives forcibly detained me, tying my hand and foot with wire and throwing me bodily into a room.

Sometime later they left the house to work in the fields and I found myself alone with the children. I called out to them and told them to take some coins out of my shirt for pocket money. Then I managed to cajole them into untying my bonds. Once free I returned in haste to my mother and reported to her all that had taken place. Since mother's passport contained complete particulars regarding her children, we found little difficulty in obtaining permission for me to leave the country. We embarked on the S.S. Karapara and after a voyage of three days arrived in Rangoon.

When we returned, Burma had just recently won her independence. I resumed working in my stepfather's shop and for a time served him faithfully and to the best of my ability.

In 1949 mother gave birth to another child and taking all her other children, went on a visit to India. Fifteen days after she left, my stepfather brought a young woman into our home. Everyday he would shower her with presents and take her to various functions and shows. I carefully noted down all the money that he was withdrawing from the shop funds and kept a record of all their social activities. Then I wrote a long letter to my mother outlining in detail all that was taking place. This letter I placed in my trunk, intending to post it at the earliest opportunity.

Unfortunately, I chose that very day to have a quarrel with the clerk in the shop. When he shouted at me I shouted right back at him. "Wait till your stepfather returns" he threatened me "I shall report you to him." This struck fear into my heart, because my stepfather had a terrible temper and was bound to punish me severely. I quickly left the shop, returned home, and after hurriedly packing some clothes, went to a friend in Thingangyun whom I knew would shelter me. In my haste I forgot all about the letter and it was left lying in the bottom of my trunk at home.

When my stepfather returned to the house and was informed that I had packed up and left in a hurry he immediately instituted a search to find out if I had stolen anything. He found nothing missing, but came upon the letter to my mother. He opened it and read the contents and his anger knew no bounds. From that day I no longer dared to go near Moghul Street.

A month later my friend in Thingangyun pointed out that he no longer dared to incur the displeasure of my stepfather by providing me refuge and requested me to leave his house. Accordingly I asked around and finally obtained a job as a servant in a Babu's house on 30th Street. Here I received no salary but was given free meals.

One day while I was washing clothes I saw an anna piece lying beside the pond. I debated whether to take it or not, but finally decided that I had gone long enough without a smoke and put the anna in my pocket.

Shortly afterwards the wife of the Babu came hurrying up and said "Did you see an anna piece lying around here somewhere?" I did not know what to say, but after a moment's hesitation replied that I had not, whereupon she called me a thief and a liar and began beating me. When the Babu returned home she reported the matter to him and he questioned me in turn. I was afraid of being beaten again so I doggedly insisted that I had not taken the money. He then started beating me very severely and I started bawling loudly. Soon a crowd had collected wanting to know what was the matter. The Babu's wife told them that I had been caught stealing some money. When they inquired how much had been taken the Babu and his wife were ashamed to admit that the amount was only one anna and so they lied and said that it was fifty kyats. The onlookers thereupon said "Then he must have been stealing for some time now, both from you and from other houses. You had better take him to the police station.

The Babu followed their advice and took me to the police station charging me with having stolen fifty kyats and I spent that night in the lock-up. This was the first time I had been in the hands of the police. I was fourteen years old at that time. At ten o'clock that night I was interrogated by the police station officer. "Is it true that you took the fifty kyats?" he asked me and when I replied that I had taken only one anna to buy a cheroot he was dissatisfied with my answer and rapped me on the wrists with a stick. He kept questioning me and beating me for most of the night but by morning he had become fully convinced of my innocence. At seven a.m. he made me polish fifty pairs of handcuffs and then released me, telling me to behave properly in future. When I told him that I was very hungry and begged him for some food he gave me four annas.

After having a meal consisting of two annas worth of rice and two annas worth of pea-soup I went around town looking for work but the Babu and his wife had spread word that I was a thief and so could not find a single opening. When I had gone two days on an empty stomach I fell in with a group of boys who were selling peanuts under the big top of the Kamala Circus on Theinbyu Grounds. When I explained my predicament to them they asked me if I would like to sell peanuts, as they did. They said that I could earn a commission of two annas for every kyat worth of peanuts sold. I was glad to accept their offer and before long was selling ten to fifteen kyats worth of peanuts a day.

Within the next two weeks or so I had become friendly with most of the members of the circus troupe. One day the owner of the circus called me into his office and asked me if I wanted a job. I said yes and he enquired what I would like for a beginning salary. I replied that I would leave that up to him and he seemed to be pleased with my answer for he hired me on the spot.

I was appointed a "Ring Boy" and given a khaki uniform to wear. My duties consisted of setting up and dismantling circus equipment in the arena. I ate together with the other members of the troupe and the food was very good.

The circus moved from Theinbyu to Kamayut and from there to Toungoo. After a week's performance in Toungoo we went on to Pyinmana. As the rail service between these two towns was not very reliable we went by road. Some of us were sent on in trucks, while others accompanied the horses and the elephants on foot. I was a member of the elephant party.

I rode on an evil-tempered tusker named Gopal with a companion and the others either walked or rode on other elephants. As we proceeded, the surrounding countryside became wilder and wilder, and soon we found ourselves in deep forest. Gopal began to show signs of restlessness, and suddenly knocked us off our perch with his trunk. Then he ran towards the other elephants and sweeping off their riders also led the whole herd of squeaking trumpeting elephants into the jungle. We quickly dusted ourselves and dashed off in pursuit, and after a prolong chase succeeded in recapturing all the elephants with the exception of Gopal. When the tusker was brought to bay he uprooted small trees and made threatening gestures with them. "Hey Gopal! It's Kanniya, Kanniya" I called out but he paid no heed. Finally, fearing that should the tusker escape the owner would be very angry and we would lose our jobs. I quietly approached from the rear and lunging forward managed to stick an iron hook into his huge flapping ear after which I hung on for dear life. This brought the huge beast down on its knees squealing for mercy and we quickly subdued and hobbled the animal.

After runs of a week each in Pyinmana, Meiktila and Pyawbwe the circus returned to Mandalay. On the way-station of Kyaukse a friend came up to me and said: "Hey Kanniya, your mother is back to Rangoon and is asking for you. She is very sad at what has happended and is crying all the time." When I heard this news I was greatly affected and from that day on began to neglect my duties. The owner of the circus noticed this but did not say anything.

Three days before the circus was due to leave for other cities I went to the owner and asked for my release to enable me to rejoin my mother in Rangoon. He refused point-blank but when I went down on my knees and placed my hands on his feet and begged him to let me go, he took pity on me and granted me permission. He also gave me one hundred and seventy-five kyats of my salalry and twenty-five kyats as train fare.

When I was paid I did not return immediately to Rangoon but visited Kyaukse, Meiktila and Pyawbwe instead, spending the money freely, with the result that when I arrived in Rangoon I did not have a single pya left to my name.

One day while I was walking down Moghul Street I glanced up at my mother's apartment. She happened to be looking at the passers-by below and our eyes met.

"Kanniya! Kanniya! Come up my son." she called out. "I don't dare to come upstairs mother" I shouted back. "Father will beat me". "Never mind that," "I will see that he does not beat you." "No, No, I can't come" I replied, but she immediately came hurrying downstairs and took me upstairs. My stepfather was sitting down to breakfast. "Why have you brought this animal into my house" he demanded. "He is my son, I cannot forsake him?" my mother replied. "If you cannot live without him you can leave the house as well" he said. My mother was greatly saddened to hear this. Realising that she could not leave her husband she took me to a friend's house on Barr Street and asked one old lady to shelter me and feed me. One month later she found me an opening as an unpaid assistant at a timber shop on West Stockade Road. At the end of nine months I had become quite useful to the owner of the shop, but he too was in debt to my stepfather, and before long I found myself out of a job again.

My mother then placed me in a job at a Chittagong General Provision Store. The proprietor was a very kind hearted man and although I was only given free meals and was not paid a salary I tried to serve him faithfully and well. However, there was another helper in the store who was stealing two or three kyats everyday from the cash box. After a year or so suspicion fell on me and I had to leave. So far as I know the thief is still raiding the till in that store.

When I related to her all that had happened, my mother was deeply affected , and finally prevailed upon her husband to accept me into their home again. In their house I had to wash all their laundry sweep and dust the floor, scour the pots and pans and also occasionally help in the shop. I could not find a single moment's spare time. My stepfather would beat me frequently and now and then would throw sticks and other objects at me.

One day, when I returned from collecting debts on his behalf I found that one kyat was missing. I do not know how this could have happened. I explained the matter to the clerk and requested him to lend me the money to enable me to make good the loss, but the clerk was the same one with whom I had previously quarrelled, and he refused. When my stepfather returned he reported the matter to him. The old man beat me till I was black and blue after which he said "Leave my house at once! I don't ever want to see your face again."

Feeling very depressed I went at once to the Pansodan Jetty and hurled myself into the water to commit suicide. However, I was seen by my friend Krishna who enlisted the aid of some Chittagonian boatmen nearby and rescued me from drowning. I was unconscious when they fished me out and after making me vomit and bring up all the water that I had swallowed, they took me to Gandhi Hospital for treatment. In the hospital I was well cared for and properly fed. Three days later I was discharged as fit.

After I left the hospital, my friend Krishna found me a job as a servant in the house of a man named Galiyarar. I was paid a salary of thirty kyats a month but had to work so hard to earn it that I decided to leave after a while. However, they kept me so busy that I did not even have an opportunity to leave the premises.

One day, fortunately, they gave me five kyats and sent me

out to do some shopping for the household. I immediately ran to a friend of Galiyarar's who lived on 31st Street and entrusted the money to him for return to Galiyarar. I explained that I no longer wished to work at that house, and begged him to help me obtain the back wages that were due me. He consented, and so I sought out Krishna, who had drawn his salary that day, and went with him to see an evening movie. I spent the night in his company, sleeping on the pavement on Moghul Street in front of the premises of Vidom & Company.

When I returned to Galiyarar's house in the morning his wife opened the door for me and when she saw who it was she and an ayah started beating me. I cried and would have jumped out of the window to end it all but did not get the chance. I also shouted at them "I did not steal your miserable five kyats. I gave it to the Babu on 31st Street to return to you" but they would not accept my word and continued beating me.

Soon a crowd collected in front of the building and some elders came up to the apartment. Galiyarar also appeared. Galiyarar's wife began weeping. I explained to the elders that I did not wish to work in this house any longer and had entrusted the five kyats to the Babu on 31st Street and that when I had come to the house to claim my back wages I had been set upon by the two women. The elders proceeded in a body to 31st Street where the Babu confirmed the truth of my story, whereupon they said to Galiyarar: "You have done this boy an injustice. Now give him his money." and I finally received my back wages in full.

When I related all that had happened to Krishna, he said, "My friend its no use trying to earn an honest living. Look at yourself. Although you have not stolen anything you have been branded a thief. You might as well get something out of it. Let us steal everything we can lay our hands on." I saw the truth of his words and agreed to do as he suggested.

Before long, I obtained a job as a peon in the Indo-Burma Trading Company. The pay was sixty kyats a month. Krishna and I decided that he should steal all he could from the house where he was employed and come and spend the night with me. I would rifle the cash box in the Trading Company and then we would run away together. Krishna duly appeared with five hundred kyats. In the early hours of the morning I broke open the cash box and found nine hundred kyats. Below the nine hundred kyats were a great many more currency notes, but since I had never stolen anything before I was afraid and my hands were trembling. I therefore took only the nine hundred kyats after which Krishna and I left the premises. We had a bad moment when we encountered a police night patrol, but escaped by running down 31st Street. We caught the bus to Thingangyun and then took the train to Pegu and Mandalay.

Three months later, when we had spent all the money we had stolen, we returned to Rangoon. The Babu from the Indo-Burma Trading Company had offered a reward of fifty kyats for our capture and one day we found ourselves surrounded by a party of about ten men. They caught hold of us and beat us up and then handed us over to the police. When we arrived at the Police station we were beaten and kicked some more by the police.

Luckily for us there was a kind hearted man among those who had captured us, and he said to the others "These fellows are poor workers like us. Why do we want to see them imprisoned? The rich always have no mercy on the poor. How do you know whether it may not be our turn next? Let us try and get them off." The others agreed and so he went to the Babu and said "Babu, we have beaten these two boys so severely that they can hardly move. The police have also beaten them so that they are more dead than alive. Please don't prosecute them any further." The Babu consented, and going to the police with them, withdrew the case against us.

Krishna and I tried to find work after this, but nobody would employ us. We took to sleeping on the pavements and eating only when we could beg a few annas from our friends. One day, I remembered Raman Chandra, a worker who had a good reputation among employers, and going to a Babu who was looking for a servant said to him "Raman Chandra sent me to you for a job." The Babu accepted this as sufficient recommendation and hired me at thirty kyats a month.

Krishna was still out of work, and I would save half my morning meal and half of my evening meal and smuggle it out to him. I did not stay in the Babu's house but slept on the pavements with Krishna.

One day, Krishna told me that he was fed up with having to do with half rations and urged me to steal from the Babu from whom we would be sure to get at least five thousand kyats. I was very reluctant to do so, since he was a kind man and I was comfortable in the job. But Krishna was insistent and to tell the truth I was also half hungry all the time, and I finally fell in with his plans.

The next morning when the Babu and his brother left for work Krishna came and knocked on the door of the apartment and I let him in. The Babu's wife wanted to know who he was and I told her that it was a friend come to help me with the housework as I was not feeling too well. While I was wondering how to go about the business of ransacking the place, the old lady solved the problem for me by shepherding all her six children into the spacious bathroom to give them their morning bath. While they were merrily splashing about I quietly bolted the door from the outside and Krishna and I quickly went through the place. To our chagrin however we obtained only twenty-five kyats in cash, a gold watch, and a German portable Typewriter.

We left the house and proceeded straight to some Chinese pawnshops where we easily disposed of the watch. However selling the typewriter was a different proposition altogether and on our second try we barely managed to escape having to leave the typewriter behind, when the proprietor telephoned for the police.

I had lost my nerve and suggested to Krishna that we go to the Indian Sadhu or Holy Man in Kanbe and pray that we be enabled to lead an honest life. Krishna was willing, and we went to see him, but there were so many people waiting to see him for the moment.

I entered a tent which the Sadhu had erected for the sick and the maimed and went to sleep after warning Krishna to lie low and not to wander about. Krishna, however did not heed my advice and started roaming arounded with a cigarette dangling from his lips. Some men from Barr street saw him and immediately gave chase and captured him. They then proceeded to beat him in an effort to reveal my whereabouts but Krishna refused to betray me and suffered all their blows in silence. Unfortunately for me these men came upon someone else who had seen me asleep in the hospital tent and I was taken anyway.

As usual I was subjected to a rain of blows on my head and shoulders after which we were taken to the Kyauktada Police Station for more of the same treatment. During the interrogation we readily confessed to having committed the burglary at the Babu's house and when we stated that we had left the typewriter at the Chinese pawnshop the police took us there in a jeep to recover the property. The Chinaman indignantly denied our story, claiming that he had never set eyes on us in his life, but we managed to convince the police officers that we were indeed telling the truth and they thereupon turned on the proprietor and threatened him with dire consequences if he did not produce the stolen property forthwith. The Chinaman finally gave in and handed over the typewriter to the police, together with a stiff bribe to escape prosecution.

When we returned to the Police Station the workers who had helped to catch us entreated the Babu not to take any further action against us, pointing out that if it had not been for them we would not have been apprehended in the first place and that we had suffered enough punishment from the blows and kicks that we had already received. The kind hearted Babu consented and in turn appealed to the police to let us go and we were released after twenty-four hours detention under Section 41 of the Penal Code.

Shortly after this, Krishna and I enlisted in the labour gangs that were being formed to be sent to Akyab. We were paid three kyats a day and given less strenuous work than the adults, and I was quite contented with the life. Krishna, on the other hand took to drink and gambling and when he was drunk became very quarrelsome. Five months later I returned to Rangoon leaving my beloved friend Krishna in Akyab.

One day, while I was walking down the street I heard someone calling my name. It turned out to be an Anglo-Indian acquaintance of mine named Mr. M. This man was always neatly dressed in European style and had many dealings with the rich Indian merchants on Moghul street. He addressed me civilly and enquired if I was free. I said yes, and he took me to a bar near the Jyoti Cinema Hall. There he stood me several drinks and during the course of the evening broached a matter that was on his mind.

He told me that he was planning to break into a shop on Dalhousie Road, and that he needed a look-out to warn him if anyone were to approach during the burglary. He wanted to know if I would be willing to do the job for him.

I was agreeable, and following his instructions, took up a position in front of the shop at ten o'clock the next morning with a bunch of balloons in my hand pretending to be a balloon seller. Mr. M soon put in an appearance and entered the building. In a short while he was out again with his pockets bugling. I followed him down the street and to an apartment near Bogyoke Market where an old ayah was waiting. There we split the loot and it turned out that my share amounted to just thirty kyats.

Not long after this I was eating in a restaurant on 29th Street when I overheard a conversation between two Indian merchants. One of them was saying;" I strongly suspect that that fellow M had a hand in the burglary at our shop." "How much did you lose?" inquired the proprieter, and one Babu replied, "One thousand and three hundred kyats. One thousand in tenkyat notes and three hundred in change." At this I know that I had been swindled by M— and from that day I began carrying a knife with which to settle account with him when we met.

For five whole days I searched high and low for M— without any success. On the sixth day however I met him walking down the road in front of the offices of the Steel Brothers' Company together with two companions. He pretended not to know me and made as if to pass but I called out to him and forced him to stop. He looked at me and turning to the others told them to go on ahead. Then he came up to me and asked, "What's the matter Kanniya, my friend?" I said; "Tell me the truth, how much did you get from the Babu's shop?" "Why, about three hundred kyats" he replied. "No, you got away with K 1300/-." I told him and explained to him how I had found out. However he did not seem unduly perturbed. "But Kanniya, you know how these people exaggerate when reporting the amounts that have been stolen from them. And of a truth, I recalled how the one anna I had picked up had been blown up into a fifty kyat theft, and much of my anger left me. But I persisted; "Even so, you obtained three hundred kyats and only gave me thirty. Was that fair?"

"Kanniya," he pointed out, "You remember I made three packets and we drew lots. Can you blame me if you picked the wrong packet?" Then he gave me five kyats, patted me on the back and promising that there would be more for me in the future, departed, leaving me quite mollified and feeling what a fine friend he was after all.

Three months after this incident, on March 24, 1954 Mr. M

sought me out again and this time tried to persuade me to join him and three others in a kidnap attempt on one of the children of the rich Indian merchants living near Moghul Street. Not having any experience in such matters I was somewhat dubious, but when he mentioned a ransom figure of K 25,000/-, K 5000/- of which was to be mine, I quickly decided that I wanted to join them anyway.

The very next day I met a sixteen year old boy named Mayaraman who lived in the Moghul Street neighbourhood and who had run away from home. I spent my last three kyats to treat him to dinner, and a movie show. That night I broached the topic of the kidnap attempt and asked him if he would care to come in with us. He was nervous at first, but I pointed out that his role in the affair would be confined to delivering one of the children to Kungyan Railway Station and that we would do the rest, he finally agreed.

On the morning of March the 26th Mr. M and Kala Maung Sein came and woke up us. They then went to a bicycle shop on Maung Taulay Street and hired a bicycle. Mayaraman was put on the bicycle and made to ride around the neighbourhood to scout for a possible victim.

At 2 p.m. a nine year old boy named Ramish returned home early from school and was accosted by Mayaraman. When offered a ride on the bicycle the boy gladly accepted and in due course was delivered at the railway station by Mayaraman. After persuading the boy to board the train on the pretext that his mother was waiting for him we arrived at Ta-wa where we got off. We spent the night at the house of a man named Ko Tun. The next day we took the boy into a hut in the jungle where Ko Tun's son Chit Maung and I were left to guard the boy, while Mr. M, Kala Maung Sein and Mayaraman went back to town to deliver the ransom note. The ransom demand was for K 25000/- to be delivered within five days to a spot in the heart of a Karen insurgent area, failing which the boy was to be murdered.

On the 28th, Chit Maung returned home, and I was left with the boy. After some time Chit Maung's brother-in-law arrived with food for us and quickly departed. At three in the afternoon we heard sounds of men moving through the woods, and then a loud command rang out. "Drop that sword!" We had been surrounded by twenty-five members of the village defense force. I dropped the sword and made to run for it, but the voice called out again. "Run, and we fire!" So I had no recourse but to stand still and raise my hands in surrender. When I saw Chit Maung's brother-in-law standing among the armed men I realised that we had been betrayed by him.

I was taken to the village Defense Force Headquarters and interrogated, but in spite of repeated beatings I refused to divulge the names of my companions. However the members of the Defense Force set up a stakeout at the jungle hut where I had been captured, and netted Chit Maung when he appeared on the road at three a.m., whistling as he came. Ko Tun also was taken the following afternoon at three o'clock.

We were delivered to the Headman of Ta-Wa and then sent on to the Kyauktada Police Station where a case of kidnapping was opened against us.

The East Rangoon Special Magistrate U Hla Gyaw passed the following judgement on us.

(1) The first accused Mayaraman in consideration of his youth, to be released and placed on probation for one year.

(2) The two coolies who delivered the ransom note to be sentenced to two years imprisonment each.

(3) Chit Maung to be sentenced to two years.

(4) Kanniya the leader in whose custody the kidnap victim was found, to be sentenced to four years rigorous imprisonment.

Two months after sentence was passed, my mother came to visit me in prison. During her visit she cried practically all the time. I felt deeply sorry for her and bitterly regretted all the grief and suffering that I had caused her. I learned later that my stepfather had stopped coming to see her altogether and that he had taken two more wives.

XV
BETWEEN TWO FIRES

*When I met Saw Htee Byan in Rangoon Central Jail in 1956
he was just twenty-four years old. He was a strapping young man with
a stocky build and a healthy complexion. His mother was Karen and
like most Karens he possessed a fine melodious voice. At my request
he sang several Karen songs while accompanying himself on the
guitar.*

*After we had grown better acquainted he readily recounted to
me the story of his life.*

*

My grandfather was a village headman in Pyapon during the
adminstration of the Hteebyan District Commissioner. Because I was
born at this time I was named *Saw Htee Pyan*. My birthplace is Amar
village which is about thirty miles away from Bogale Town, Pyapon
District. My father's name is Ko Hla Shein and my mother's is Ma
Ngwe Khin or Naw Yon Mu. My father is pure Burmese hailing from
Upper Burma and my mother the daughter of a Karen Headman. My
grandfather, U Po Byù was well known in the area, being a headman
who had been awarded a double barreled shotgun by the government
for meritorious service. My father was a carpenter. He had come to
repair the paddy barges belonging to my grandfather and had fallen in
love with my mother. Grandfather approved of the match, and had
them married with proper ceremony.

I was the first child to be born of their union. My grandfather
doted on me and named me *Htee Pyan* after the District Commissioner of that name. This official was named *Htee Pyan* ("the umbrella
returning" Commissioner, because practically all accused who
appeared before him were sent to prison and only their umbrellas
returned home).

Amar was a Karen-Burmese village of about two hundred houses. While it boasted two Buddhist monasteries, it had no secular school. When I was five years old my grandfather died and we moved to a village about fifty miles away called Kanyin-tabin. This village also had about two hundred houses and there were both Karen and Burmese families in the village. However, the Burmese far out-numbered the Karens, of whom there were only twenty households. My father set up shop as a carpenter, while my mother opened a small school to teach Karen and Burmese.

About the end of the Japanese occupation I was ten years old, and had acquired three sisters. The person charged with the anti-Japanese Resistance in our area was a man named Bo Kyaing. This officer attacked the Japanese prematurely and in reprisal they came and razed our village to the ground. We had to flee to another village thirty miles away called Myit-nga-hseik. Father set up a general provision store there, in partnership with five friends from Ohn-bin-su village near Pyapon. My mother no longer taught school and I had to attend the Karen school in the village.

Grandfather had been a pastor in the Karen Christian Church. Before he died he had managed to convert my father from Buddhism to Christianity and my father now became a pastor as well. He could deliver very fine sermons both in Burmese and Karen.

At about this time the political situation took a turn for the worse, and one day hearing gunshots, I ran home to find that rebels from the Karen National Defense Organization had attacked our home. Father had managed to escape unscathed, but of his five Burmese friends, two were found dead inside the house while the remaining three were found outside also dead from gunshot wounds. Mother was inside the house weeping. The rebels pointed their rifles at me and shouted, "How about you? Do you want to be a Burman or a Karen?" Only by replying that I wanted to be a Karen was my life spared. They then carried off all our property, leaving only our clothes, some salt, and a basket full of rice.

The K.N.D.O rebels then left after ordering the village militia to deliver the corpses to Pyapon. The militia had been organised by the government, but its members were Karen. They took the bodies to the Pyapon police station, where they reported that my father Ko Hla Shein had murdered his partners and had absconded.

Meanwhile my father was hiding out in the jungle without food and water, not daring to approach the vicinity of human habitation because the story the K.N.D.O rebels had spread had turned everyman's hand against him.

I travelled to Pyapon to see my father's younger brother who was a Lieutenant in the Army and related the true story to him. My uncle came with me to view the corpses to make sure that father was not included in their number. Then he accompanied me back to the village, together with a squad of soldiers to search for him.

Some young cowherds informed us that a man had been seen sleeping at nights in the cemetery of nearby Char-gyin village, and making our way there quietly, we saw that it was my father. "Father! Father!" I called out to him, but he took fright and ran away. However the others immediately gave chase and finally succeed in capturing him. Since he was wanted by the authorities my uncle had to surrender his own brother into custody.

After a month's investigation the government published its findings declaring that my father was innocent of his crime, and that the K.N.D.O's and the militiamen were the murderers. The relatives of the victims wanted action to be taken against the real culprits, but they could not be found. Ever since the news broke that my father was innocent, the militiamen had refused to obey all summonses issued for their appearance at the Pyapon police station. Father was released from custody, but he no longer dared to return to the village, Mother also was afraid to join him. Their separation dates from this time. I remained with my mother. I hear that father is living in Rangoon but I know neither his address nor his prevent occupation.

*

Although father had been a pastor he had put me in the Buddhist monastery school. He said that he wished to see his son brought up as a Buddhist. Accordingly, during the Japanese occupation I was novitiated together with seven other boys in a grand ceremony.

*

When I returned to the village with mother the Karen insurgents asked me: "Are you going to stay here, or do you wish to move to a Burmese village?" I had to reply: "I would like to stay in this village please."

To make both ends meet, my mother had to sell the five cows that we had left, and with the proceeds buy a garden plot which we worked for the next two years. At the end of this period the Communists attacked, Myit-nga-hseik village and so we returned to our original home in Amar village where we took up catching shrimps for a living.

Having grown up in Burmese villages I could not speak Karen when I was young. On going to live with my mother and her relatives my cousins found out that I could not speak Karen and ostracized me as a Burman. Occasionally I would be punched and kicked by the older boys. When my mother complained to her brother about this he summoned all of us and explained to the other children that I was the son of their aunt and a Karen also and that I did not know their language because I had been brought up in a Burmese village. He urged them to help me learn Karen instead of ill-treating me because I could not speak the language. He then turned to me and said that from that day on I was not to speak a single word of Burmese and that every time I did so I would be caned, and also fined one anna. For a long time I found great difficulty in communicating with the people around me. My uncle would talk to me in Karen asking me to fetch something and I would have to rush to my mother and ask her in a whisper what it was that he wanted. Then I would run to him and say in Karen: "Here it is, uncle." His face would be wreathed in smiles and he would rattle off some long sentences, none of which I understood.

Finally my mother had a brillant idea and had me enrolled in the Karen village school. The schoolmaster was a very sympathetic and kindly soul, and took my education in hand. I worked very hard under his tutelage, with the result that now I can speak and read Karen more correctly than any of my cousins.

When I reached manhood I was enlisted as a member of the local security force set up by the Karens to maintain law and order in our area. I was appointed leader of a platoon. One day a member of my unit got drunk and held up a Chinese merchant from Bogalesetsu. On my next trip to this town to deliver dried shrimps I was stopped by armed police and searched. They also proceeded to my hut where they uncovered a revolver and three cartridges. I was arrested straightaway. At first they charged me with the unsolved murder of a man named U Than Maung, but I could prove my innocence on that charge and so it was dropped. However the Chinese merchant came forward to accuse me of robbery and the magistrate sentenced me to two years imprisonment.

I have been working as a carpenter in the prison when I have served my sentence I intend to go back to shrimping, at which I can earn up fifteen kyats a day.

Being a Karen-Burmese I often encounter armed partisans of both sides. The Karens want to kill the Burmese and the Burmese feel that the only solution is to exterminate the Karens. It saddens me greatly to hear such talk. Having witnessed how my father and his friends had had to suffer at the hands of Karens holding narrow sectarian views I find it difficult to forgive the Karens. On the other hand I have seen how cruel the Burmese can be and that makes me embittered at them. When Karens suffer I feel resentful and when Burmans suffer I feel resentful also. Sometimes I wonder whether racial strife and civil war will ever be ended.

*

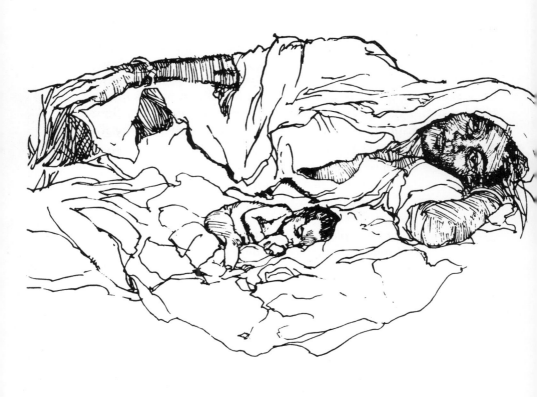

XVI
THE ENTREPRENEUR

While serving out my three year sentence in Rangoon Central Jail I used to practice golf everyday for a period of over one and a half years. There were four or five avid golfers in the prison with me at the time, and they took great pains to help me improve my game.

We had five "browns" instead of "greens" constructed on the soccer pitch and used to play several rounds every day on this miniature golf course.

Our golf course adjoined the No.3 Cell Block, and Maung Aung Kyaw Tun, a young prisoner of Arakanese extraction from that block would watch us with great interest as we played round each day. When ever we lost a ball in the rough he would join in the search and help us locate it. Before long he began to caddy for us and in no time we had promoted him to "brown-keeper" receiving a monthly allowance to which we players all contributed.

When I made enquiries regarding the circumstances that led to his imprisonment, this is what he had to relate:

*

I was born on Sagu Island, Ramree District. My parents U Shan Pu and Daw Saw Myaing were cultivators. There were eight children born to my parents, of whom I am the fourth eldest. We owned the seven or eight acres of land that we cultivated and the two pairs of oxen that we used for ploughing the fields. On this land we managed to produce over one hundred baskets of paddy annually.

On Sagu Island there were altogether nine villages. Our village, called Ye-Gaung-Chaung was one of these and comprised about eighty houses. There was no secular school in the village. At one time an attempt had been made to recruit a schoolmaster and open a grade school but after a while the school master went on leave and has not re-appeared to this day.

The education of the village youth was thus left entirely in the hands of the monks in the monastic school. There were two monks and three noviatiates in the village monastery, and they took sole charge of teaching the rudiments of learning to the sixty or so pupils who were enrolled.

All the schoolchildren were males, since it was not considered fitting for females to enter a monastic school. This has been our tradition ever since I can remember. My mother does not know how to read or write while my father reads with great proficiency. My sisters do not read at all, while my brothers can do so fluently. I do not think that in the whole village there were not more than ten women who were literate.

At the age of 8 I was sent to the monastic school. I had to sleep at the monastry and accompany the monks on their morning round for almsfood. I had my morning and noon meals at the monastery and my evening meal at home. When I returned home in the evening I had to feed the 8 cows which my parents possessed and help with other household chores.

When I was thirteen years old I was novitiated together with my two elder brothers into the Buddhist religion. My brothers, who were 15 and 17 years old remained in the monastery for 2 months while I donned the robe for only 7 days. I continued to study in the monastic school until I was 14 years of age.

When I was 15 years old the insurrections broke out. My aunt who was quite well off dared not remain in the village any longer and so moved to Kyaukhpyu taking me along for company. In town my aunt opened a general provision store in partnership with a few friends. This store was named the Shwehintha Stores, and dealt in textiles, monks' requisites and in jaggery of palm sugar. At the age of 12 I was already carrying boxes of jaggery weighing 28 viss to and from the dockyards.

The work was very strenuous, and my aunt had a very sharp tongue. After a year or so I could stand it no longer and left her to return to my parents' home. A year later my aunt followed me to the village and prevailed upon me to come back with her to town. Once back in her house however she resumed scolding and beating me as before, but following my mother's advice I pretended not to hear her when she did so.

When I was 19 my aunt put me on the plane to Rangoon. At Mingaladon Airport I was met by a merchant named U Hpyu Daung and taken to No. 15, 29th Street which housed the offices of the Thamegga Wahneiksa Trading Company. I lived on these premises for about a year while acting in the capacity of purchasing agent for my aunt's store. My job was to buy oil, jaggery, monks' requisites, textiles and toilet articles and ship them to Kyaukhypu.

At the end of the year, when the accounts were all in it was found that the Shwehintha stores had sustained a loss. The six shareholders in the company grew dissatisfied with the state of the company affairs and fell out among themselves. My aunt and her husband wrote to me informing me that they had decided to form a separate company under the name of "The Thamar-Warneissa-Trading Company" and that I was to act as their agent, in addition to my duties as purchasing agent for Shwehintha stores.

At the end of the next six months the Thamar-Warneissa Trading Company had turned a profit of six thousand kyats, while the Shwehintha Stores continued to run at a loss. This prompted the other shareholders in Shwehintha to accuse me of neglecting the affairs of their company and paying all my attention to Thamar-Warneissa. This led my aunt and her husband to propose a merger of the two companies, and the other shareholders accepted the offer with alacrity.

Some time later a trader named Aung Shwe Tha from Myebon in Kyaukhpyu District and four companions came to put up at the company offices. At the same time a trader named Tun Myat Aung from Taunggup and seven others were also sleeping on the premises. Since there were three of us who lived there permanently, there was not enough sleeping room for everyone in the 25' × 50' space available. Accordingly I went and spent the night in the house of a friend of mine on 38th Street.

When Aung Shwe Tha returned to Kyaukhpyu he reported to my uncle that I did not sleep on the office premises but made it a practice to sleep out. My uncle immediately sent me a letter reprimanding me in very harsh terms.

My cousin also wrote me a letter but did not blame me ; only enquiring into the actual circumstances of the matter. I wrote a reply to my cousin out-lining the facts and adding that the company offices kept me so busy that I had no time for any sort of night life in Rangoon.

Not long after this my uncle arrived in Rangoon to set up a partnership with Tun Myat Aung of Taung-gup in the dyeing business. A month later he returned to Kyaukhpyu. Shortly after this a trader named Bo Mya U from Kyaukhpyu arrived in Rangoon and after inquiring into the costs of dyeing requested me to buy five bundles of yarn, have them dyed, and send them urgently to him in Kyaukhpyu. Accordingly I went and purchased the yarn, leaving the goods in the store, and went to Tun Myat Aung and handed him the purchase voucher, explaining the circumstances and asking him to take delivery of the yarn and make arrangements to have it dyed.

Tun Myat Aung fell into a rage at this, pointing out that I was his junior and that it was insolence on my part to order him around. He wrote a letter of complaint to my uncle, and my uncle immediately sent me an abusive letter in which he placed the blame squarely on me. He then brusquely informed me that he was severing all my connections with the dyeing concern, and that I was never again to show my face at its premises on Ahlone Road.

About a month later an uncle of mine who lived in Kanbalah village near Hainggyi Island in Bassein District came to visit us in Rangoon. My brother was at that time studying in Rangoon as a monk at the Mingala Rama Monastery on Stockade Road. When the time came for him to leave this uncle tried to persuade the two of us to accompany him back to his village to visit our relatives. When my brother excused himself on the ground that he had already made arrangements for a trip to Mandalay my uncle insisted that I at least go along with him. I explained that I could not leave the company affairs unattended, but he would not take no for an answer. Accordingly I decided to combine business with pleasure and going to some merchants whom I knew, explained the situation to them and took K 2000/- worth of textiles on credit for sale in my uncle's village.

In Kanbalah village I managed to sell K 600/- worth of textiles, after which I fell sick. The fever had not left me one and a half months later, when my uncle from Kyaukhpyu arrived. He had been informed by Tun Myat Aung that I had absconded with the textiles. I explained that I had been too sick to move, but he would not believe a word of what I said, neither would he accept my Kanbelu uncle's assurance that I was telling the truth.

I managed to sell a few more textiles and then gave K 825/- to the Kyaukhypu uncle. He bought some glazed pottery jars and shipped them back to Kyaukhpyu, sending me along on the sampan, sick as I was, to look after the consignment on the voyage.

When I arrived in Kyaukhpyu I explained everything to my aunt and taking the remaining textiles, returned to my parents village to try and dispose of them. However, the people in that village were quite poor and could not afford to buy much, so I went on to Patin Island and exchanged K 300/- worth of textiles for 3000 pieces of thatch which I managed to sell in Kyaukhpyu for K 550/-. This money was confiscated by my uncle, as was K560/- which I made by selling 30 men's coats and 20 women's coats sent from Rangoon. He also impounded K 500/- of my money which I had kept with him for safe keeping as well as some money that I had entrusted to my brother who ran a beauty store in Kyaukhpyu Bazaar.

Seeing that I was unemployed in Kyaukhpyu the brother who worked in the Shwehintha stores asked me if I would like to return to Rangoon to resume my work as purchasing agent for him. My uncle strenuously objected, but I paid my own air passage back to Rangoon and took up my duties there.

A short while later he wrote a private letter to a woman named Ma Kyin Hmwe in Rangoon telling her that I was no longer trustworthy, that she should not entrust large sums of money to me, and that he no longer considered me a foster son. When Ma Kyin Hmwe showed me his letter I was greatly saddened and felt even more rejected. My room-mate Ko Kyaw Zaw from Kyaukhpyu wrote to my uncle trying to placate him, but his letter only made matters worse and made the old man detest me all the more.

As it was becoming increasingly clear at this juncture that I had only myself left to rely on and that I had better start earning my own living. I approached a textile dealer and managed to get K 1000/- worth of textiles from him for sale in Kanbalah village and other neighbouring villages in the Bassein district.

In a little over a month I managed to sell over eight hundred kyats worth of textiles, and when I returned to Rangoon I had the money and about four hundred kyats worth of textiles left with me. The merchant who had let me have the goods on credit had in the meantime visited the office in Rangoon, and not finding me there had concluded that he had been cheated and has reported the matter to the police.

I arrived in Rangoon at 7 a.m. and went straight to a person in Kyeemyindaing to collect a debt. When I returned to my house at 2 p.m. I was met by officers from the Pabedan Police Station who took me into custody. During the interrogation they accused me of having cheated the textile dealer. I replied that I had not stolen the goods but had received them on credit whereupon they demanded that I produce documents to that effect. When I pointed out that it is not customary to give receipts for goods taken on credit they said I was lying and hit me several times in the face.

The next day I was released on bail owing to the efforts of some friends of mine and I immediately sought out the dealer and informed him that I had K 800/- in cash as well as some goods left in hand. I offered to repay him K 500/- immediately and the rest of money in a short while if he would only withdraw the charges against me. He refused point-blank, saying that I would have to repay the entire amount at once. This I was unable to do.

I had been arrested on the 5th of May, 1955. On the 17th of September the Third Additional Magistrate sentenced me to one year's rigorous imprisonment. I did not have any money with which to appeal the decision and was brought here to serve my sentence.

I do not know what I shall do when I am released from jail. I plan to look up a friend who lives near Whitehall. He has visited me two or three times here in prison and I think he is a true friend.

*

Maung Aung Kyaw Tun was released from Rangoon Central Jail about ten months before me. I had managed to arrange for him to be given an apprenticeship with a newspaper publishing firm. He had worked hard at the job, and by the time I met him again he had been given full employment and promoted to the post of printer's assistant.